ALL ABOUT
CREDIT

Questions (and Answers) About the Most Common Credit Problems

Deborah McNaughton

DEARBORN™
A **Kaplan Professional** Company

This publication is designed to provide accurate and authoritative information in regard to the subject matter covered. It is sold with the understanding that the publisher is not engaged in rendering legal, accounting, or other professional service. If legal advice or other expert assistance is required, the services of a competent professional should be sought.

Editorial Director: Cynthia Zigmund
Managing Editor: Jack Kiburz
Project Editor: Trey Thoelcke
Interior Design: Lucy Jenkins
Cover Design: DePinto Studios
Typesetting: the dotted i

Published by Dearborn
A Kaplan Professional Company

Printed in the United States of America

99 00 01 10 9 8 7 6 5 4 3 2

Library of Congress Cataloging-in-Publication Data

McNaughton, Deborah, 1950–
    All about credit : questions (and answers) about the most common credit
  problems / Deborah McNaughton.
      p.   cm.
  Includes index.
  ISBN 0-7931-3153-7 (pbk.)
    1. Consumer credit—United States.   I. Title.
HG3756.U54M359   1999
332.7'43—dc21   99-19950
                                                CIP

DEDICATION

To my husband, Hal, who is my greatest cheerleader; my daughters Tiffany, Christy, and Mindy; my two sons-in-law, Mike and Kyle; and my grandchildren Austin and Alexis.

To the thousands of individuals I have counseled, who never gave up and found answers to improve their financial situations, gaining new hope and direction.

CONTENTS

PART THREE / Your Financial Future

PREFACE

Credit and finances are concerns that constantly play in our minds. "Can I qualify for a mortgage to buy a house?" "My expenses are higher than my income. What can I do?" "The bill collectors are after me. How can I stop them?" "My credit report is ruined from a divorce. Help me!"

Most people, at some time in their lives, experience some type of financial hardship. Addressing the problems quickly and correctly can make all the difference in the world between solving problems and having them remain ongoing. Unfortunately, most people tend to bury their heads in the sand and hope the problems will disappear.

One of the first questions interviewers ask me is why people get into the financial problems that they do? The answer is that most adults and young people lack education on how the credit system works. Very few schools teach this topic and most parents never teach their children the importance of handling credit and money. Unfortunately, we often learn about credit and finances the hard way: negative entries can remain on our credit reports for up to ten years.

Daily I am inundated with questions from callers and clients who are facing difficult situations and need answers today. I have been on more than two hundred radio and television talk shows where the telephone lines are jammed with individuals seeking answers to their problems.

This book is a compilation of questions that I have been asked either on the airwaves or at my office. The stories that I share with you in this book are true (the names have been changed). I have discovered that everyone has a story. Some problem details may be different from yours, but frequently the solution is the same.

It is amazing how often we find ourselves feeling as though we are the only ones in the world with financial problems or facing financial challenges. You're not alone, and not being alone with a problem somehow makes us feel better.

This book is a sequel to *The Insiders Guide to Managing Your Credit* because the questions being asked are followed by direct answers.

The following pages provide information on all areas of credit. The book is divided into three sections. Part One covers all areas of obtaining credit. This part will answer your questions if you want new credit or a mortgage, never had credit, women and credit, overcoming credit denials, unsolicited and preapproved credit cards, and understanding the credit reporting agencies as well as your personal credit reports. Part Two discusses credit problems. This part will answer your questions about credit and charge card problems, marital problems, handling financial problems after a divorce or death, collection agencies, communicating and negotiating with creditors, cosigning, and bankruptcy. Part Three helps you build your financial future. This part answers questions on getting out of debt, repairing your credit report, and reestablishing your credit after financial problems or a bankruptcy. There also is a chapter on common miscellaneous questions.

In my more than fourteen years in the credit consulting business, I have heard stories that have been heart-rending. Credit and financial problems can happen to anyone at any time.

Everyone facing financial challenges needs hope—and a plan. Without a plan, there is no solution. It is my sincere desire that anyone who reads through the chapters of this book will gain knowledge. With knowledge and a plan, you will be empowered to come to a quick decision and solve whatever problem you are facing.

PART

1

KEYS TO OBTAINING CREDIT

CHAPTER 1

QUALIFYING AND APPLYING FOR CREDIT

Qualifying for credit is an art. It is important that you know what you are getting yourself into before you complete a loan application. You need to know what the credit grantor is looking for to get an approval. You also need to know what type of credit and terms you are applying for. Too often individuals are shocked when they are issued credit and the terms are different from what they thought.

Before applying for any line of credit, do your homework. Read the fine print on the loan application. Screen the bank, savings and loan companies, or credit unions before applying for credit cards. The differences in interest rates, loan fees, annual fees, late fees, and payment requirements can be vast.

Interest rates can be calculated on a daily basis (interest charges start accumulating when a purchase or charge is made), or on a pro-rated basis (no interest is charged until a balance remains in a new billing cycle, which usually includes a 25-day grace period).

A credit grantor will review the length of your employment, your previous credit, whether you own or rent your home, if you have a checking and savings account, and your credit rating before making a decision to approve (or not) your application. Using the information you give on your credit application, the credit grantor will assign a certain number of points to each category. This will give you a credit score. The scoring is discussed later in this chapter. If the score is high enough, and your credit report is satisfactory, your application will be approved. Each company has its own credit criteria.

Be selective on whom you give your information to. Do not give any information to anyone over the telephone unless you have verified his or her legitimacy.

TRUE STORY: IT HAPPENED TO ME!

Several years ago my husband, Hal, and I decided to lease a car. We were undecided on which car we wanted. One afternoon I overheard Hal talking to someone on the telephone. He was giving the individual on the telephone his name, address, and Social Security number. I quickly started flagging him not to give that information out. It was too late. Hal said the person asking for the information needed it for their records in order to find us a car. Subsequently, we decided to delay getting a car until a later date.

Several months later I requested a copy of our credit report from one of the major credit reporting agencies. As I was reviewing the credit report I discovered four inquiries from banks that were never authorized by either Hal or me. Knowing what I did about unauthorized inquiries, I called the individual whom Hal had spoken with regarding the car and asked who gave their company authorization to run our credit report? I quickly informed the company that I knew my rights under the Fair Credit Reporting Act and that they ran a credit report without our written or verbal authorization. I gave them 14 days to remove these inquiries from our credit report. This individual started to stammer and said he didn't know how he could get the lenders to remove the inquiries as his company gave the lenders permission. It didn't matter to me how they removed it; I knew my rights. All four of the inquiries were removed within the 14 days.

Excessive inquiries within a six month period will cause many applications to be denied.

The moral of this story is to never give out your name, address, or Social Security number to anyone unless you know what they intend to do with it and they are a reputable company.

STABILITY

Q. *What qualifications must I have to get a line of credit?*

A creditor is looking for the three Cs of credit: capacity, character, and collateral.

The capacity to pay is determined by your employment as well as the length of time you have been employed. Creditors want to know about your income, bonuses, and any commissions you may receive. Included with capacity are your expenses and how many dependents you have. Creditors then determine how much you can afford to borrow or how high a credit limit you can qualify for.

The credit grantor evaluates your character by reviewing your credit history and paying habits. It gets this information from Experian (TRW), Trans Union, and/or Equifax credit reports. These are the three major credit reporting agencies. Also reviewed is the length of time you have lived at your current address. If you have been at your current address less than two years, you will be asked to list your previous address. If you move frequently, you may not appear stable. The status of owning or renting your home is also reviewed.

When a credit grantor is reviewing your collateral it wants to see what assets you have other than your income. Assets could be viewed as a savings account, investments, and property you own.

The more stable you appear, the better the chances of an approval on your application.

EMPLOYMENT

Q. *What type of employment history is a credit grantor looking for?*
I have been employed at my present job for 1½ years.

The credit grantor is looking for at least two years of employment at your current job. If you have been at your present job less than two years, you will need to supply your employer's name, your position or title, your line of work, and the dates of your current and previous employment. If you have no time lapses in your employment history and your line of work has not changed, you have a chance of a loan approval providing all other qualifying factors are good.

If you had a lapse of time between jobs, the credit grantor may not approve your credit application.

Another thing a credit grantor is looking for is the number of years you have been employed in your current line of work. If you have changed your line of work and have worked in your new field less than two years, you may not be approved.

CREDIT REPORTS

Q. *When a credit grantor reviews my credit report, what is it looking for?*

A credit report tells a complete story of your paying habits, how much you owe, if you are overextended on your accounts, and what your balances are. It also will reveal your current address, previous address, and occasionally your employer.

A credit grantor is making sure you have revealed all the pertinent information you have listed in your loan application. If there is any derogatory information listed in your credit report such as charge-offs, collection accounts, slow payments, delinquent payments, tax liens, judgments, or bankruptcies, your application may be denied or further explanations may be required.

Always get a copy of your credit report before you apply for credit. There may be errors you need to correct before proceeding with your application. An incorrect report may result in your application being denied.

CREDIT SCORES

Q. *How does a credit score affect my qualification for credit?*

If a credit grantor subscribes to each of the credit reporting agencies, it can have access to a special credit scoring system that the credit reporting agencies reveal in their analyses of your credit reports. This is known as a FICO score. A score can range from 0 to 900 points. Using a combination of factors, the FICO score will reveal if you are deemed creditworthy. For example, suppose you are in the market for a new car. The car dealer would request a copy of your credit report from a credit reporting agency. It will reveal your paying habits and FICO score. If you have a FICO score of 700 points you would be automatically approved for your car loan without having to supply any further documentation. If your FICO score falls below 700 points, the dealer may require more documentation from you to get the loan approved.

Whether for a car loan, mortgage, or credit card, each lender has its own criteria in determining what FICO score you should have. In addition to the FICO score, if there is any derogatory information on your credit report, you will be asked for an explanation. If your debts are too high when added to the new purchase or line of credit, your application may be denied.

As an individual, you can't get a copy of your FICO score from the credit reporting agencies; this is only provided to the business subscribers. If you want to know what your FICO score is, you must apply for credit through a mortgage company, auto dealer, or merchant that subscribes to this service. These companies are under no obligation to reveal the score to you, however many will upon your request.

Another way a credit grantor evaluates your application with scoring is by assigning a certain amount of points to specific categories. For example points would be assigned for the following: marital status, number of dependents, whether you own or rent your home, years of employment, credit history, monthly obligations, age, years at your current residence, years at your previous residence, occupation, monthly income, and other factors. The points are totaled. If you fall within their range, you will be approved.

BANK ACCOUNTS

Q. *Do I have to have a checking or savings account in order to get credit?*

A creditor wants to feel secure knowing that you have money in a bank account, especially as you need to make payments with a check or direct withdrawal system.

You don't necessarily need to have both a checking and savings account. However, you are rated higher with the credit scoring in qualifying if you have both. Be sure to list the name, address, and account numbers on the application whenever asked. Specify which account is the checking and which is the savings account.

LOW INTEREST CREDIT CARDS

Q. *Is a low interest rate cards hard to qualify for?*

Yes. A low interest rate card requires that you have a good payment history, with no derogatory information, and that you are not overextended. The creditor will look at your job stability and income and the length of time you have lived at your current address.

Before applying for a low interest rate credit card, call the credit processing department and find out what the creditor's criteria is for qualification. Find out what credit reports they run.

Prior to applying, get a copy of your credit report from all three credit reporting agencies: Experian (TRW), Trans Union, and Equifax.

If you know prior to making an application to the creditor that you fit the criteria the creditors are looking for, then follow through with the application. If you don't fit the criteria, make whatever improvements are necessary and apply at a later date.

RENT OR OWN

Q. *Does it matter when applying for credit if I rent or own my home?*

A credit card company will look more favorably at your application if you own your home. However, if you rent it will look at how long you have lived at your current residence. If you move frequently, your application will be denied. A creditor will look at your past two years of residency. Some creditors may look as far back as five years. If the credit grantor feels you are stable—regardless of renting or owning your home, the application will be approved.

The credit grantor wants to feel secure that should you not make your payments, it has a means of collecting the debt. Most credit cards are unsecured. In some states, a creditor's only recourse to collect the debt is to get a judgment against you which would secure the payment with your home when you either sell or refinance the property.

If you are applying for a mortgage, a lender will look at your credit history and how long you have lived at your present address. The creditor will verify length of residence through your landlord or mortgage lender. Whether or not you pay your rent or mortgage on time is reviewed closely because it may indicate how you will pay your new loan.

If you are trying to rent a home or an apartment, a credit report may be requested. If there are problems listed on your report, the landlord may increase the required deposit.

If you are upfront about any credit problems, many creditors will work with you or show you what to do to reapply in the future.

INTEREST RATES

Q. *How is my loan interest rate calculated? Why do some of my credit cards offer a grace period, while others do not?*

Before completing a credit application, read the disclosure of terms located somewhere in the application. The disclosure of terms will list the annual percentage rate (APR). For example, your APR may be 21 percent. To figure out the total cost of a loan in dollars, multiply the monthly payments by the total number of months of the loan. From the total payments subtract the total amount borrowed to see how much you are paying in interest.

For a credit card, some creditors calculate interest on a daily basis. That means that interest charges begin to accumulate as soon as a purchase or charge is made. Other creditors calculate interest on a pro-rated basis, giving you a grace period. That means no interest is charged until the billing cycle. The grace period could be 25 to 30 days from the purchase date. You can repay the amount you charged in full during the grace period with no interest charged.

The best cards to use would be those that have a grace period. You get free use of the money during the 25 to 30 days before the statement is due. The way to take full advantage of this form of payment is to pay the total balance off each month.

Always review your credit card application to see what the cost will be. If there is no grace period I would suggest you look for another creditor who offers one.

If you always pay your credit card balance in full, you want a grace period and no annual fee; you don't care what the APR is because you will never pay it!

CHAPTER 2

CREDIT DENIALS

Nothing is more frustrating than applying for a home or car loan, credit card, or other line of credit and having your application denied. There are several reasons why a person could be denied credit. It could be because of insufficient income, too brief a period of employment, too many credit obligations, negative and derogatory credit report information, no checking or savings account, and so on.

When you have been turned down for credit, the creditor must notify you in writing within 30 days of the denial. In the denial letter, it must indicate the reason for the denial and the name and address of the credit reporting agency used to review your credit report.

Once you have received the letter of denial, you have 60 days to request a free copy of your credit report from the credit reporting agency listed. (The reporting agencies are required to give a free report to anyone who was denied credit based on their reports.) Don't try to get a free report from a credit reporting agency that is not notated in the letter. The credit reporting agencies have a record of the inquiry in their system from the creditor who denied you credit.

The letter of request for your free credit report should include your name, address, Social Security number, and birthdate. Attach a copy of your letter of denial with your request letter. You should receive a copy of your credit report within 14 days. Review the credit report. Contact the creditor who denied you credit to see exactly what the problem is and how to resolve it. Once you know the problem is resolved, you can reapply or go to a different institution.

BETTY'S STORY

While I was being interviewed on an Ohio radio station, Betty called in with a question regarding a purchase she recently made. She asked: "I was recently turned down by my bank for a car loan. I have excellent credit. I was very upset about being turned down so I went to another bank and was approved. Was I being discriminated against by the first bank?"

My answer was: "The first bank that rejected your credit application is required to send you a letter of denial stating the reason your application was denied. This letter must be sent to you within 30 days of your rejection.

"Different creditors have different criteria in qualifying you for credit. Each bank, savings and loan, credit union, and credit card agency has a credit scoring system that it uses. It assigns a certain amount of points for each entry on the application. If the points are not high enough, the application will be denied. When the second bank approved your application, it may not have had as strict guidelines for qualification as the first lender did and that is why you were approved for the loan by the second bank. Also some banks are more aggressive than others in soliciting customers.

"When qualifying for credit there are other things besides your credit report that the lender is looking at. Your income, job stability, loan amount, and assets all play an important part when qualifying for credit.

"I do not believe that you were being discriminated against. I believe the first bank had stricter qualifications than the second bank, forcing you to look elsewhere."

JOB INSTABILITY

Q. *My husband and I are trying to purchase a car. I am a home-maker. My husband has been out of work two times within the past three years. He is employed now. We keep getting turned down for a car loan. What is the problem?*

Lenders look for several factors when making an evaluation for granting credit. One big factor is job stability. If a lender can't establish two years of continuous employment, it may decline the application. Because you are a homemaker with no income, the lender can't look to you to support a stable income.

If your husband went from one job to another without an interruption, and the job was in the same line of work, the lender would consider approving the loan. If he changed his line of work and started a new job, this could present a problem.

In the future, keep records of the name, address, telephone number, dates of employment, and salary from all previous employers. (In these days of closings, mergers, and buyouts, keeping pay stubs could be a good idea.) This information will allow the credit grantor to verify information and approve your application.

TOO MANY CREDIT CARDS

Q.   *We have always taken great pride in our good credit rating. Recently we applied for a credit card and they declined our application. We have several credit cards that we always pay on time. Why did this happen?*

When a credit grantor is reviewing your credit application, they also are reviewing your credit report and your income. If you have several credit cards with outstanding balances the credit grantor will evaluate your debt to your income. The credit grantor will calculate your monthly fixed payments, such as your rent or mortgage, automobile, bank installments, charge/revolving accounts, child support, your proposed loan payment, and any other expenses you report. Once the monthly expenses are calculated, a calculation of your gross monthly income (before taxes) is tabulated. Your salary, spouse's salary, commissions, bonuses, alimony, child support, retirement income, and any other source of income is calculated.

To calculate the debt-to-income ratio you would total the monthly payments (expenses), and divide the monthly payments by the total gross monthly income. This will equal your debt ratio. If the ratio is over 50 percent, the credit grantor may not approve the loan.

Your problem may be that you have too much credit and not enough income. If you have open accounts with no balances, it will be counted against you. The credit grantor will assume that in the future you may use the unused credit and run up your debt ratio. Close all open accounts that you are not using. Write a letter to each of the creditors requesting that they permanently close the account. If you are in possession of the credit card, cut it up, and mail it with your letter cancelling the account.

Sometimes accounts shown on your credit report may have been closed but they are still showing up as active accounts. This also is misleading to the credit grantor. Make sure that the creditor is contacted and the account reflects closed.

UNLISTED TELEPHONE

Q.   *Recently I applied for a credit card. The credit card company sent me a denial letter. I called the company back to see what the problem was. The person I spoke with said he couldn't verify my telephone number. Our telephone number is unlisted.*

   The individual I was talking to said he would call me right back. He called me right back at the telephone number I gave and said I was approved. What was that all about?

Many credit card companies will not approve a credit card or line of credit if your telephone number is unlisted.

The reason is that there is a higher risk of not being able to find you if you default on your payments. Many credit applications now request a copy of your current telephone bill with your telephone number listed on it. This is cross-referenced to your name and address.

If your telephone number is unlisted, to eliminate a problem when applying for credit, attach a copy of your telephone bill with the application. This will eliminate a delay or denial of your original request.

Many applications require that you list references such as relatives or friends. This is not to see who you know. It is to use as a reference and contact if you quit making your payments and your line of credit goes into default. If you have changed your telephone number or address and the creditor can't locate you, the individuals listed on the application will be contacted to try and get information on your whereabouts.

NO ACTIVE ACCOUNTS

Q. *I have had great credit in the past. I paid all my accounts off two years ago. I went to apply for a new credit card and was turned down. The letter the bank sent me said "No previous bank borrowing within the last 24 months." What does that mean?*

Most lending institutions and credit card companies are looking for your past 24 months' payment history. The past 24 months is a good indicator of how stable your financial situation is and how you pay your bills.

The credit grantor is reviewing your credit report to see what accounts you have had in the past. By paying off all your credit obligations, no payment history will be reported on your credit report. The credit report will indicate the last date of activity.

If there have not been any payments made on any accounts within the past 24 months to show a payment pattern, many lenders will decline the application.

When applying for credit, it is important to do your homework and analyze what a lender will look for in qualifying you for credit.

Paying off your credit cards is great. It would be wise, however, to keep one or two accounts open and pay the balances off each month. That way there will always be a payment pattern should you seek additional credit.

SELF-EMPLOYED

Q. *I have been self-employed for more than four years. I am having trouble getting new credit. Why is this happening to me?*

Individuals who are self-employed have greater difficulty in getting credit than individual who have an employer. The reason is that your income is harder to verify than someone who is an employee.

Most self-employed people write off numerous expenses on their tax returns, which off-set their incomes. You may have a steady cash flow, but a creditor reviewing your 1040 Federal tax return may think the income appears very low due to your write-offs on your Schedule C IRS form.

Being self-employed has added risk to the lender because your income flow is not consistent. Many people who are self-employed have had poor credit history because their income is not stable.

To get credit approval, you must be self-employed at least two full years. Make a photocopy of any 1099 Forms that you receive and attach the forms to your application. This will boost your income. If you are contracted with any specific companies to do work for a specific time, list the company on the application and the income you are receiving.

If your company is incorporated, make sure the income you are receiving can be verified with your paystub or yearly W2 forms. Do your homework before applying for any credit. Find out what the criteria is from the lending institution before you send in your application. If you can provide the required documents, don't hesitate to apply. If you fall short, gather the necessary information that will be required before you reapply.

BANKRUPTCY

Q. *Five years ago, I filed for a bankruptcy. I was told that I could get new credit without any problem. I have been trying to get new credit but I am constantly being turned down. What happened to the fresh start that I thought I could get?*

Unfortunately most people think that once they file for bankruptcy their problems are over.

A bankruptcy is a public record that is recorded and picked up by the credit reporting agencies.

It has been said that some creditors will give you credit because you can't refile for a bankruptcy for at least seven years. However, most individuals I have talked to have found this to be untrue.

Creditors want some distance between the time the bankruptcy was discharged to the time of application. Most lenders will not consider looking at an application for at least two years from the date of discharge.

If there has been any negative activity on your credit report since the bankruptcy you will be denied credit.

Several new companies are now offering lines of credit for individuals who have gone through a bankruptcy. Many of these companies have access to mailing lists of people who have filed bankruptcies. If you receive an application, review it carefully to determine what the fees are. These types of credit are usually very expensive with high fees and high interest rates.

TAX LIENS

Q. *Two years ago the Internal Revenue Service filed a tax lien against me. All of my credit is good except for the tax lien that appears on my credit report. I need to refinance my house and have been denied the loan. What can I do?*

A lien that has been filed against you is recorded at the county clerk's office and becomes a public record. A lien could be a tax lien, mechanic's lien, or judgment. When you have a lien filed against you and still owe money on it, most lenders will not issue you any type of credit.

The lien represents an unpaid bill that has been attached to your property. If you have a first mortgage on your home and try to sell or refinance your property, the lien must be paid off prior to the sale or refinance, or through the escrow. The reason it must be paid is because if the mortgage loan is paid off, the lien would move into first position. A loan company trying to put a new loan on the property is not willing to be in second position to a lien. The risk is too high for the company. The lienholder could force a sale of the property to enforce payment of the debt.

The best solution is to make an agreement with the IRS to make installments or make an offer-in-compromise to reduce the amount you would owe. Another suggestion would be to see if the lienholder would subordinate its position to enable you to get a new first mortgage. You should seek the advice of your accountant or tax attorney.

Once you have solved your tax problem and paid off the tax lien, it is important that you get a release statement from the IRS. This must be a written statement indicating that the lien has been paid in full. Make sure this is recorded with the county clerk's office. Mail a copy of the release to all the credit reporting agencies so their records can be updated. This will make it easier for you to get credit in the future.

EXCESSIVE INQUIRIES

Q. *Why are excessive inquiries hurting my chances of getting credit?*

Five or more inquiries within a six-month period may hurt your chances of establishing new credit. Credit scoring is a big factor in qualification. Too many inquiries within a short period of time will lower your score.

For example, if you were trying to get a car financed through Ford, and they ran a credit report and denied your credit application, an inquiry would appear. You then go to Chevrolet, and they run a credit report. The Chevrolet dealer notices that you have just come from Ford, which may cause a denial of your credit application based on the denial from Ford. You then go to Toyota, and they run a credit report on you and see that you have been to Ford and Chevrolet. Toyota may question your credit report and deny you credit based on the inquiries by Ford and Chevrolet. This can go on and on with inquiries. The more you have listed on your credit report, the more questionable you are to the creditor.

The best way to avoid excessive inquiries is to be prepared when applying for credit. Have an updated copy of your credit report on hand to show the merchant. If you are applying for a car loan or a line of credit where you can personally show the credit grantor a copy of your credit report without authorizing the company to run a report on you, do it. Excessive inquiries could be avoided. If the company acknowledges that you would be approved, allow the company to run a new credit report on you. The company will have to in order to complete the loan.

If the company determines you would not be approved you have saved an inquiry from being posted on your credit report.

Inquiries are automatically removed from your credit report two years from the date they were made.

NO CREDIT HISTORY

Q. *I have always paid cash for everything. Now I am trying to get a credit card and I can't. Isn't it better to pay cash than to use credit?*

Paying cash for everything is a good habit, although paying only with cash will not help you establish credit. A credit grantor looks at your credit report to see your paying habits. By using cash you show no payment history.

In today's society you cannot function without establishing credit. Without established credit you would not be able to purchase a home or car unless you paid all cash. You can, however, have credit without having debt by paying off your credit card balances in full when your statement comes due. This is a good practice, plus it would be reported on your credit report as payments made on time. This will result in establishing a positive payment history and can be beneficial when trying to qualify for a mortgage.

No credit is just as bad as having negative credit. You will be denied credit either way. See Chapter 3 for ways to establish credit.

CHAPTER 3

FIRST TIME CREDIT

A typical question is, "How can I get credit if I never had credit? I'm turned down for credit because I never had any, but no one will give me a chance."

It is a vicious cycle. However everyone has to start somewhere. Many young adults are faced with these issues as well as individuals who have sworn off using credit and pay cash for everything. Careful planning and strategies can get you the credit you need.

Without a major credit card you can't rent a car or reserve a hotel room or airline tickets.

There are several ways to establish credit: secured credit cards, merchant cards, cosigners for credit, friends or relatives, and automobile dealers. (Each of these will be explained later in this chapter.)

It is important that you understand the seriousness of paying back your credit cards or any loans that you may receive. You never want to be late making a payment. If you find that your payment is going to be late, call the creditor and explain your situation. Find out how many days late you can be before it goes on your credit report. Don't wait to make a double payment the next month. If the past due payment rolls into the next billing cycle, most creditors automatically report a late payment on your credit report.

When you are trying to establish credit, the credit grantors are looking for six months to two years of credit and payment history. They will look at your income and length of time you have lived at your residence.

Never apply for more credit than you need. Too many open and unused accounts will hurt your chances of getting new credit. Once you have established new credit, make sure that you review your credit report once a year.

JACK'S STORY

Jack had never had credit. He was 20 years old and in college. When he replied to a credit card offer, his application was denied. The letter indicated that he had a negative entry on his credit report. Jack was confused, because he never had a credit card or any credit that he was aware of. He requested a copy of his credit report and was shocked to see a collection account listed on it. The collection account was the only item on the report. Jack never knew he had a collection account until he saw it on the credit report.

Jack contacted me to see what I could do to help. With the collection account listed on his credit report, he would never be able to get credit. No one would give him a chance.

I instructed Jack to call the collection agency and find out what the bill was that they were reporting. The collection agency indicated it was a past doctor bill that had not been paid. Jack had never received a bill from either the doctor's office or the collection agency.

Jack contacted the doctor's office regarding the past due bill and made arrangements to pay the bill off. The doctor's office agreed to have the collection agency remove the derogatory information from his credit report because no statements were ever received.

Once the collection account was removed, I had Jack complete an application for a secured credit card from a bank offering a secured credit card program. He deposited $250 into a savings account with the bank and was issued a secured credit card with a limit of $250. He was on the road to establishing new credit.

NEVER HAD CREDIT

Q.   *How can I establish credit when I have never had any?*

One good way to establish credit is through a secured credit card. A secured credit card is a VISA or MasterCard that has been secured by a deposit to a bank offering this type of program. For example, if you were to open an account with a bank offering this program, and deposited $300 into an account, the bank would give you a VISA or MasterCard with a credit limit of $300. You would be paid interest on this account, however when you use your VISA or MasterCard you will be charged interest.

This type of credit is good to help you establish new credit or re-establish credit if you have had credit problems in the past, including a bankruptcy.

As you use the card, you will receive a monthly statement. Pay the balance off in full or at least make the minimum payment on time. As the payments are received, the bank will report the activity on your credit report. This is important because you are building a payment pattern for future lines of credit. Many banks will issue you an unsecured credit card after you have been with them for 18 months. The key is making the payments on time.

With a secured credit card, there may be an application fee and/or an annual fee. More and more banks are offering this type of program. Contact your local bank to see if they offer any secured credit card programs. You also can look in the business section of your newspaper to see if they have information on which banks offer secured credit cards.

COSIGNING MY DAUGHTER'S CREDIT CARD

Q. *My daughter just graduated from high school and received a credit card application. In the application it asked for a parent's signature. Would this be a good idea?*

I am always leery about any application that asks for a cosigner. The reason the credit card company is asking for a parent's signature is to make sure the payment will be made and that you, the parent, are guaranteeing the line of credit. In other words, if your daughter runs up the bill and doesn't make the payments, the creditor can come after you to collect. This is reported on your credit report as well as your daughter's. If there are any delinquencies or defaults on the account, your credit report will reflect this.

I would not recommend that you cosign for your daughter. Most high schools don't educate their students on the importance of credit and how the credit system works. The risk is too great for your credit rating to be destroyed by a young person who doesn't understand how the credit system works.

The best way to teach your daughter about credit is to help her get a secured credit card. Have her save $300 and deposit it into a bank that offers secured credit cards. The bank will issue her a credit card with a $300 limit, secured by her deposit.

By having her get this type of credit, she will begin to understand how the credit system works and build a good payment history. After she has done this for one year, she will be in a better position to apply for an unsecured credit card.

COLLEGE STUDENT

Q. *This is my first year of college. I've never had a credit card. There are several credit card companies at school that are trying to solicit me to get one of their credit cards. Is this a good idea?*

Colleges are full of companies offering VISA, MasterCard, and American Express cards to students.

The danger is that most of the students will get these cards and use them as power cards. For example, a student who has just got a credit card may want to impress his peers. He may opt to buy dinner for a group of friends, or use the credit card to make purchases such as stereos, televisions, CDs, and so on. These purchases are being made with the mentality that he only has to pay $25 per month. Wow! What a deal! The dangerous thing is that when reckoning day comes, the statement arrives and there are $500 worth of purchases. The interest rate is 21 percent. If the student never makes another purchase using the credit card and makes the minimum payment each month, it would take approximately seven years to pay off and cost him $404.64 in interest charges. And if the student is ever late or defaults on the payments, it will be reflected on his credit report for up to seven years.

I believe a college student should get one credit card, providing she keeps track of her purchases and pays the balance off in full each month.

That is showing responsibility and will reflect as a good payment history on her credit report, which can help in the future.

USING A FRIEND OR RELATIVE FOR CREDIT

Q. *I am trying to establish credit for the first time. Someone told me it would help to have my name on a friend or relative's credit card. How does that work?*

There are two ways that you could use this technique in trying to establish credit in your name.

Once a credit card is issued to an individual, frequently the card issuer allows the cardholder to request an additional card in another person's name. Ask your friend or relative to obtain a card in your name.

You could tell your friend that she can keep the card because you will not be using it. Ask her to request that the credit grantor report the payment pattern on your credit report. That way a positive credit rating will be established for you. If for some reason the friend or relative cannot make the payment, have her let you know so you can help. Otherwise your credit report could be hurt by nonpayment.

If your friend or relative doesn't mind you using the credit card, make sure you keep track of all the purchases you make and make the payments on time. It would be better if the credit card was only used by one person so your purchases would not be confused with the original cardholder. Have the statement sent to your friend or relative. Make the payment to the credit card company on time. That way your friend or relative will feel secure.

Once you have established a good payment pattern on your credit report, apply for your own credit card. Have your friend or relative cancel the card with your name on it. If there is still an outstanding balance, make sure you continue to make the payments to reflect a good payment pattern.

MAJOR CREDIT CARD VERSUS MERCHANT CARD

Q. *I have never had a credit card in my name. A local merchant indicated that I could apply for its credit card. Would this help me establish credit for the future?*

A merchant's card could be good providing it reports your payment history to the major credit reporting agencies. If the merchant is not a subscriber to the credit reporting agencies such as Experian (TRW), Trans Union, and Equifax, your payment history to that particular store will not be reflected. It basically would be a waste of effort for establishing credit.

When applying for credit for major credit cards, department store cards, and any type of lending institution, a credit report is always run to evaluate your paying history. Make sure the merchant is a subscriber to the reporting agencies.

Once you have a merchant card and have established a good payment history, you should apply for a VISA or MasterCard. Look for a low-interest credit card. Most merchants charge high interest rates.

When you have one or two VISA or MasterCard's, cancel your merchant and department store credit cards and only use the low-interest credit cards. Most establishments accept VISA and MasterCard.

ATM VISA/MASTERCARD

Q. *I have a checking and savings account. I was issued an ATM card to use as a VISA card. Will this help me with my credit report in establishing credit?*

Using your ATM card as a charge card will not help your credit report. It won't be reported as a credit card.

An ATM card is not a credit card. The amount for any purchases that you make with your ATM card with the VISA or MasterCard insignia is directly taken from your checking or savings account. There is no statement sent to you at the end of the month to make payments on the purchases because the money was automatically taken from your account and paid to the merchant.

By using your ATM VISA card you can keep better track of your purchases. It can be used the same way a credit card would be used for reservations and purchases, but there is no billing other than the automatic transfer of the funds from your bank account to the merchant's account.

FIRST-TIME BUYER AUTO PROGRAMS

Q. *I have seen advertisements for first-time buyer automobile purchases. Will this help me establish new credit?*

Any time you respond to an advertisement for a first-time buyer purchase for an automobile, always read the fine print. Make sure you understand how the program works.

The car dealer may require a larger down payment or deposit for the car. You also will probably pay a higher interest rate than you would from a financial lender.

Make sure the loan company that the car dealer uses to place your loan is a subscriber to the credit reporting agencies. If they are not, don't get the car. It is important that your payment history is reported to the credit reporting agencies.

If you complete the purchase and pay on the car for at least 12 months, you can shop around to another lender that offers a lower interest rate and have the new lender refinance the car.

Because you have been making your payments on time and show a good payment history, you have a good chance of refinancing the car and also establishing new credit with a major credit card.

CHAPTER 4

WOMEN AND CREDIT

Every woman, whether married or single, should have credit in her own name. Should anything ever happen to her spouse and the family credit is in the husband's name, she may not be able to then establish credit for herself. This is especially true if she is a homemaker who is suddenly widowed or divorced with no job or income.

The Equal Credit Opportunity Act was designed to stop discrimination against women. She may not be denied credit just because she is a woman or because she is married, single, widowed, divorced, or separated. As long as she shows that she is creditworthy and falls into the guidelines of the credit application, she can't be discriminated against.

When she applies for credit, she does not have to use Miss, Mrs., or Ms. with her name. She can chose to use her married name, maiden name, or a combination of both surnames (for example, Mary Williams Smith).

If she has recently married, she should contact each of her creditors and give them her new married name and other pertinent information. Have her creditors update their credit files and notify the credit reporting agencies of the changes.

If she divorces and decides to use her maiden name, she should ask each of her creditors to change her name on their accounts. Once the creditors' records are updated, it is important that they notify the credit reporing ing agencies. Obviously, if she had some negative accounts in her husband's name, I would strongly advise not to have them changed into her name; her credit report would be ruined. The idea is to try and build a credit report without any derogatory information.

JENNIFER'S STORY

A Controlling Husband

I was on a radio talk show, "For Women Only." When the host opened up the telephone lines for questions, Jennifer called in. She whispered, "I can't talk very loud because my husband is in the other room and I don't want him to hear me. We have been married for eight years. Before I got married, my husband had me sign a prenuptial agreement. He has credit cards and a checking and savings account that he uses in his name only. He has never set up a joint account with my name on it for either a credit card or bank account. I have to ask him for any money that I need to run the household. I feel very insecure with our finances. My husband never tells me how much money we have or the status of our financial situation. We are having marital problems. Is there anything I can do to protect myself and establish credit in my own name?"

Jennifer's husband was trying to control her by not allowing her to spend money without his consent. Her marriage was in trouble. The first thing I recommended to Jennifer was to open up a checking account in her name. Any extra money she could save and put aside needed to be put into her checking account.

The second thing I instructed Jennifer to do was get a copy of her credit report from all three credit reporting agencies. It was important for Jennifer to see if there was any payment history on her credit report. Perhaps her mortgage was being reported on her credit report without her knowledge. Any positive item that appeared on her credit report could be used to help Jennifer establish new credit in her own name.

Once Jennifer received all three credit reports, I advised her to apply for two different credit cards. I instructed her to apply with a local merchant or department store for a credit card. Once she received the credit card from a merchant in her own name and made payments for at least six months, she needed to apply for a VISA or MasterCard. Where the application asks if the account is for individual use, or joint, Jennifer checked "individual." An individual account holds the applicant solely responsible for payments on the account and authorizes her as the sole person to make purchases with the credit card.

When she was approved and received the credit cards, I suggested that periodically she make small purchases that she could pay off when the bill came due. This would reflect a good payment pattern on her credit report.

If Jennifer and her husband were to get divorced, Jennifer would be in a much better position than she currently was by planning ahead and getting her credit established, rather than trying to do it later.

HUSBAND'S CREDIT

Q. *The credit cards that I use are in my husband's name. Because I am using his cards, do I need to get any credit cards in my name?*

Yes! Every married woman should have at least one or two credit cards in her name. This is to protect yourself should your husband die or you get divorced. If something happened to your husband and all the credit was in his name, you could have a difficult time establishing new credit for yourself. Your credit report could show "no record found," which can be interpreted as having bad credit.

Because the credit cards are in your husband's name, you are only a user on the card. Sometimes the credit card company will reflect this on your credit report, however don't count on it. Check your credit report from all three of the credit reporting agencies to see if any of the accounts you are using are listed on your credit report.

If you apply for a credit card while you are married, you do not have to have your husband as a cosigner or be listed jointly if your income is high enough to meet the stated requirements.

YOUR CREDIT CAN REBUILD HIS CREDIT

Q. *My husband and I went through a major financial crisis. The credit cards that my husband was using became delinquent and*

are now being reported on his credit report. I have two credit cards
that are in my name only and in good standing. Can I put my
husband on my account? Would this help him rebuild his credit?

Yes! Many times a wife is able to help rebuild her spouse's credit report by adding him to her credit card account. You can add your spouse as a joint applicant. The credit card company would then request his Social Security number and income information. Because you are the primary applicant, you are responsible for all the payments.

If all the payments have been made on time, this will be picked up by the credit reporting agency and reflect as a positive entry. The more positive entries on your husband's credit report, the easier it will be for him to reestablish his credit.

It still is advisable for you to have a credit card solely in your name. You never know when you may need it for an emergency.

NO RECORD FOUND

Q.   *My husband died several years ago. All the credit cards were in*
his name. I applied for a new credit card and was denied. I made
all the payments on these cards but my credit report says "no
record found." What can I do to get new credit?

Check to see if any of the credit cards that your husband had were joint accounts. If they were, contact the credit card company and instruct it to report this to the credit reporting agencies. If none of the accounts were held jointly, you will have to start all over in reestablishing your credit.

Go to your local bank and see if it offers a secured credit card program. A secured credit card is a VISA or MasterCard that you get from a bank after you make a security deposit. I would recommend that you get two secured credit cards and charge small amounts each month. Pay the full balance off every month. Your good payment history will be reported on your credit report. Make your payments on time. Within six months to one year, request that the bank issue you an unsecured credit card in place of the secured credit card.

This is not an overnight process. If you continue to make your payments as agreed, however, you eventually will be able to get new credit.

CHILD SUPPORT AND ALIMONY

Q. *When I apply for credit, can I report my child support and alimony payments as income to qualify?*

Absolutely! When reviewing your application, the credit grantor must consider any income—whether it be full-time or part-time employment, child support, and alimony.

I have a friend who is divorced with three children. She is working full time and receives child support and alimony. The child support and alimony payments are higher than her income.

Several years ago she applied for a mortgage for a new home. Her wages were not sufficient; however, with the child support and alimony, she was able to qualify for the home and complete the purchase. Always include child support and alimony when applying for credit or a loan.

NEW MARRIED NAME

Q. *When you get married and have a new last name but have the same Social Security number, can you get new credit?*

Whether you are married or single, the credit reporting agencies use your Social Security number as an identification source. If you apply for new credit under your married name, the Social Security number would be cross-referenced and reported with your maiden name. This could cause your credit report to be merged together with your married and maiden names. All of your accounts would appear on one report.

It is important that you notify the creditors of your name change so that creditors can update their records, which would be reflected on your credit report. Once creditors are notified of the name change and their files are updated, they will report your active accounts and any activity on your accounts to the credit reporting agencies using your new name.

JOINT ACCOUNT AFTER DEATH OF SPOUSE

Q.   *My husband died and we had some joint credit card accounts. Will I lose the credit cards?*

A joint account is the only type of account that protects you against being closed because of the death of a spouse. The Equal Credit Opportunity Act states that a creditor cannot automatically close or change the terms of a joint account solely because of the death of a spouse. The creditor may ask you to update your credit application or reapply if the initial acceptance of the application was based on all or part of your spouse's income and the creditor has reason to suspect your income is inadequate to support the line of credit.

If a creditor requires you to reapply, it must give you a written response to your application within 30 days. While the application is being processed, you may use your line of credit with no interruption. If, for some reason, your application is turned down, you must be given the reason in writing.

The chances of the creditor closing your account are very slight, as long as you continue to make your payments on time and do not exceed your credit limit.

CHAPTER 5

UNSOLICITED AND PREAPPROVED CREDIT CARDS

Credit card companies are always looking for new customers. They use whatever enticement they can to draw you to their companies. They may offer you a low interest rate credit card or give you incentives such as airline miles, discounts on certain items, long distant telephone privileges, reestablishing credit, and so on.

People have problems because they don't read the fine print. There are usually specific things that you must do to comply with the credit card company's terms. A lower interest rate credit card offer would require you to move your higher interest rate credit card balances to the new card. If you don't follow their guidelines, the credit card company can increase the interest rate on the new card to an interest rate higher than you were paying on your old cards. The lower interest rate is usually temporary, leaving you to move your balances again when another new low interest rate credit card is offered. Unless you are making your payments over and above the minimum payment requested on the low interest rate card, it still would take you several years to pay your balance off.

A problem that you can run into when accepting too many credit offers is acquiring too much debt. It is easy to lose track of what credit cards you have by adding several new credit cards. If you don't cancel the credit cards that you have and are not using, this will hurt you when you are trying to establish new credit. By not keeping track of what credit cards you presently have, you risk the danger of being overextended and sinking into more debt.

Consumer advocates blame banks and other credit card offerers for inundating consumers with more than 2 billion credit card solicitations, tempting creditworthy and not-so-creditworthy individuals to live beyond their means.

JOANNE'S STORY

JoAnne and her husband had recently married. Both came from previous marriages and JoAnne's divorce had not been amicable. Her credit report had been damaged as a result of disputes over who would pay the credit card bills. It was hard for her to get new credit.

When JoAnne received a preapproved credit card for 5.99 percent interest rate, she was thrilled. She transferred all her high interest rate credit card balances to the new low interest card.

Several months went by and JoAnne made it a point to pay her credit card payment on time. One month, the bank did not receive a payment by the due date. As a result, the credit card company increased her interest rate to 22 percent, which was higher than the original interest she had transferred her balances from. The payment skyrocketed!

The small print of the application stated that the company could increase the interest rate should a payment be received late. There was no recourse for JoAnne except to make the payments.

When JoAnne contacted me, she was in the market to consolidate her debts with a home equity loan. She explained her situation with this high interest rate credit card. By doing a debt consolidation loan, she was able to save hundreds of dollars per month and pay off her high interest credit card.

TOO MANY SOLICITATIONS

Q. *My husband and I keep receiving unsolicited preapproved credit card offers. How did we get on these different mailing lists?*

There are several ways that your name is distributed to credit card companies looking for new business. Believe it or not, the credit reporting agencies issue names of individuals to mailing companies who request certain categories for solicitation of credit cards.

Companies will outline the type of individuals they are seeking to solicit for these preapproved credit cards or applications. For example, if you have excellent credit, your name may be given to banks and credit card companies offering low interest rates. If you have had past credit problems, you would be solicited by companies who are offering secured credit cards or unsecured credit cards with high interest rates.

Other ways your name will be shared with others are magazines you subscribe to, ordering merchandise through mail order, contributing to charitable organizations, and credit card companies who you have accounts with. These organizations sell their membership or customer lists to mailing list companies. This is another source of income for these companies. Lists of names sold to mailing list companies are periodically updated.

Be careful whom you give your name to. Find out prior to your order if your name will be placed on a mailing list.

DENIED A PREAPPROVED CARD

Q. *I received an announcement stating I had been preapproved for a credit card. I turned in my application and was denied. What happened?*

Most of the preapproved applications are not what they appear to be. People who receive these preapproved offers rarely read the whole letter, nor do they read the full application.

If you read the small print, it will usually have a disclaimer stating that the preapproval is subject to acceptance of the application. If you read the small print in the application, you will discover it states that you will be approved subject to a credit report review and verification of information from the application.

There could have been several reasons you were denied the credit card. Your credit report may not reflect a good credit history. Your income may not be high enough. The credit report may show too much debt. The length of your current residence may not be long enough.

A preapproved application will use the same qualification factors as if you had solicited the application yourself. Never complete any application unless you have read every word in the letter and application. This will help you avoid sending in an application that you know would be turned down and eliminate an inquiry being placed on your credit report. Too many inquiries on your credit report can hurt your chances of new future credit.

STOP SOLICITATIONS

Q. *It seems like daily I am getting unsolicited preapproved credit card offers. How can I stop this?*

You can contact each of the three credit reporting agencies to request that they remove your name from all mailing lists. The addresses are: Experian, P.O. Box 2106, Allen, TX 75013-2106, Trans Union, P.O. Box 7245, Fullerton, CA 92834, and Equifax Options, P.O. Box 740123, Atlanta, GA 30374-0123. Include in your letter your name, complete address, Social Security number, and signature.

To reduce the number of direct marketing mailings, you can write to: Direct Marketing Association, Mail Preference Service, P.O. Box 9008, Farmingdale, NY 11735-9008. To request that your name be removed from Direct Marketing Association member lists, include your complete name, full address, Social Security number, and signature. If you write to the Direct Marketing Association, you'll be removed from its lists for three years.

You should contact your existing credit card companies and other creditors to demand that your name be removed from their mailing lists.

REGULATIONS OF PREAPPROVED CREDIT CARDS

Q. *I heard there was a new regulation regarding a person who receives a preapproved credit card offer being turned down. Are there any reasons I could be turned down?*

The Fair Credit Reporting Act recently made changes allowing creditors to reject your preapproved credit card application if they conclude that you are unemployed or your income is not high enough. Formerly, the company was required to make an offer of credit. The preapproved credit card usually had a high interest rate or a very low credit limit.

The Fair Credit Reporting Act allows creditors to consider any substantial changes in your financial condition. This could be a sudden drop in your income or a sudden increase of debt. If anything should occur between the time you make application to the time of the review of the application you can be denied.

Many credit institutions are replacing their preapproved offers with invitations to apply. It is always wise to read all the fine print on any solicitation to apply for credit. Many times the offer is not what it appears to be.

INQUIRIES ON CREDIT REPORTS FROM PREAPPROVED CREDIT CARD COMPANIES

Q. *I heard that when a credit card company sends a preapproved offer that it doesn't show up on your credit report as an inquiry. I have received several preapproved applications. I requested a copy of my credit report and there were at least 15 inquiries made by companies that I never heard of. I did recognize a few companies who had sent me a preapproved letter. Are all these inquires going to hurt me?*

Credit reports are very confusing because they list inquiries in two separate ways.

Inquiries made from creditors you applied to, or have current accounts with, will reflect inquiries on your credit report. The date, name of the creditor, and reason for the inquiry is reported. These inquiries are viewed by anyone who receives a copy of your credit report. Inquiries will stay on your credit report for two years from the date the inquiry was made. Excessive inquiries will hurt your credit score and can cause you a denial of credit.

Inquiries made from creditors for purposes of offering preapproved credit cards or for other solicitations are not shown to other companies viewing your credit report. The inquiries will only show up on the version of the credit report that you receive.

An inquiry made from a preapproved credit card company will not affect your credit rating or credit score.

Each credit report that you request on yourself will have an explanation of the inquiries and will separate the inquiries that were for preapproved credit cards or other solicitations, and those inquiries for purposes of obtaining new credit.

CREDIT SOLICITATIONS AFTER CREDIT PROBLEMS

Q. *Several years ago I went through a divorce. My ex-husband ruined my credit. I have been trying to reestablish my credit with a secured credit card. Recently I received an offer for an unsecured credit card with a $500 credit limit. I got the card without any problems. By getting these solicitations, does this mean that my credit is looking better?*

If you are receiving unsolicited credit card offers, you have begun to rebuild your credit history and enough time has passed since your previous credit problems.

Many companies are looking for people like yourself who have had past problems but have rebuilt their credit histories. Usually the interest rates are higher and low credit limits are offered; however it is a way to reestablish your credit.

SECURED CREDIT CARDS

Q. *Several years ago I had severe financial problems. I have not applied for credit, assuming that I would be turned down. Recently I have been getting offers from companies stating I am preapproved, but they want me to deposit money into their bank to get the credit card. What is the catch?*

Secured credit cards are an excellent way to reestablish credit. It also is a good way to control your credit card charges because you are using your own money.

A bank offering a secured credit card requires that you deposit a certain amount of money into a savings account at its bank. In exchange for the deposit, you will be issued a VISA or MasterCard. The bank would pay you interest on the money you deposited into your savings account. The amount that you deposited would be your credit limit. Any purchase or charge that you made with the credit card would be charged interest. For example, your deposit may be $500. A VISA or MasterCard would be issued to you with a credit limit of $500. You would receive interest on the amount you deposited, however you would be paying interest on your balance. To avoid paying interest, pay the balance off every month.

With a secured credit card, you will pay an annual fee as well as a one-time set-up or processing fee. The interest rates are high, but it is a good way to establish or reestablish your credit.

Some individuals who have not had credit problems will still opt to have a secured credit card. They may deposit the maximum amount allowable into a savings account, draw interest on the balance, use the credit card, and pay the balance off each month. Many people find this is a good way to keep control of their own money and earn interest while doing it.

QUALIFICATION FOR AN UNSECURED CREDIT CARD WITH PAST CREDIT PROBLEMS

Q. *Four years ago, I became late on several credit cards. They were all charged off. I never paid them back. I haven't tried to get new credit, knowing that my credit report was bad. I have begun receiving letters with applications offering credit cards to people with past credit problems. They are not requiring a deposit. Are these offers any good?*

Many banks have found a new way to help individuals with past credit problems reestablish their credit with unsecured credit cards. The VISAs and MasterCards being offered have a low credit limit and extremely high interest rates. The banks do not offer a grace or float period, which means the interest begins to incur once the purchase is made and continues on a daily rate until the balance is paid off. The initial processing fee is very high and there is an annual fee. Usually the initial processing fee and annual fee is added to your credit card once you have an approval. For example you are approved for a $500 credit limit. The processing fee is $149 plus an annual fee of $50. Your credit card would be charged these fees leaving you with a balance of $199. The interest would begin immediately until you paid the balance off. It's a great moneymaker for the bank.

Banks offering this program have certain criteria they look for prior to approving your application. You can't have any credit problems or blemishes on your credit report at least six months prior to making the application. You will need to include a copy of your pay stub and a copy of your telephone bill listing your telephone number with your application.

These types of credit cards are good for individuals who don't want to set up a secured credit card with a deposit. It is a way to reestablish your payment history. Once you have reestablished your credit history, pay the credit card off and try for a lower interest rate credit card.

CHAPTER 6

QUALIFYING FOR A MORTGAGE

The American dream is to own a home. There are several types of loans available to qualify for a mortgage. There are loans that you can qualify for with low down payments such as 3 percent down.

It is always best to be prequalified for a loan by a lender or mortgage company prior to looking for a home to purchase. By getting prequalified you will know what the maximum loan amount is you can qualify for, and approximately what your monthly payment would be. If there are any problems you need to take care of, such as errors on your credit report, you have the opportunity to resolve the problems before you put a deposit on a home. Once you find the home you want to purchase, you want to be able to get a preapproval on the loan as soon as possible.

Getting a new home loan or a refinance on your present home is basically the same criteria in qualification. A residential loan application must be completed. Other documents that will be reviewed are credit reports, an appraisal, verification of deposits in your bank, verification of your employment, tax returns for two years, and pay stubs. Once all the documents are in, the file is reviewed. A loan package is prepared and sent to an underwriter (lender) for an approval. If there are any problems in your past, it is a good idea to inform the loan processor in advance.

Many individuals who have gone through a bankruptcy or financial problems are now able to qualify for mortgages. There are lenders, known as "subprime lenders," who will make loans to individuals with past credit problems. Their interest rates are higher than the traditional lenders, but it is a good way for individuals to reestablish their credit. Assuming real estate prices continue to rise, even with a higher interest rate, the cost would be lower than paying a higher price for the property in the future. My suggestion to clients who have to go to the subprime lenders is to refinance their home after two years. The goal is to have reestablished credit and have a good payment record to qualify for a lower interest rate.

WALK AWAY FROM HOME SCAMS

Q. *I have a mortgage that is upside down. I owe more money than the house is worth. I have seen advertisements of a company who says they can take over my property. The company indicated if they took over our loan it would not affect our credit rating. Is this a good move?*

No! There have been many companies popping up offering to assume the mortgages for individuals who have fallen behind in their payments or are upside down in their loans. These companies will charge you a percentage of the loan or a flat fee to take over your property. For example the company would charge you $1,500 to sign over your property to them.

The company would have you sign an agreement stating they are not responsible for making the payments and that you will transfer over the title of your property by a quitclaim deed. The company can dispose of the property any way that it deems necessary.

The objective of such a company obviously is to collect an up-front fee. The company has the property and usually stops making payments. It may try to find a buyer for the property. The buyer who would fall prey to this scheme is one who is unable to qualify for a mortgage due to past financial problems. The buyer would then pick up the payments on the home after paying the company a down payment. The company would then quitclaim deed the property to the new buyer. Most lenders will call the loan due and payable in full if they find out that the originator of the loan is not the one making the payments.

The problem with all of this is that you are still on the original loan. When the company quits making payments on the loan, your credit rating with the mortgage company is ruined.

Once the new buyer has the property, the buyer will make the payments on the loan to the company who sold it to them. The payment is higher than the one on the original loan and a higher interest rate is charged. The company would then make the payment to the mortgage company and keep the difference of the original loan payment and the new payment. This is known as a wraparound loan or AITD (all inclusive trust deed).

The only way you will be released from your obligation to the mortgage company is if the new buyer refinances the loan in his or her own name.

If the company does not find a buyer for the property, it will go into foreclosure. This will appear on your credit report and hurt your chances of getting a new mortgage for many years.

The company that is making you this offer would also suggest that you purchase another home prior to signing over your current home. This is especially attractive if you are not late on your mortgage payment, but owe more on your mortgage than the appraised value of the property. By doing this you would be secure in your new home because your credit rating is good. However, if the company doesn't continue to make the loan payments on your original home, a foreclosure will occur, hurting your credit report and any future credit or purchases.

These companies are rip-offs. You would be better off trying to ride out the storm and sell after property values increase.

The state attorney general's office has been investigating these companies for misleading the public.

FICO SCORES FOR QUALIFICATION

Q. *I am applying for a mortgage. I was told that I had a good FICO score. What does this mean?*

When you apply for a mortgage, your credit report is run. In order to get your FICO score, the lender must be a subscriber to the credit reporting agencies and get FICO scores from them.

Credit report (FICO) scoring is a statistical means of assessing how likely you are to pay back a loan. A score is based on the information listed in your credit report. The score measures the degree of risk you represent to the lender. The score does not include your income, assets, or bank accounts. They don't use age, sex, race, color, religion, marital status, occupation, homeownership status, length of time at present address, or zip codes to calculate a score.

Fair Isaac Credit Bureau Score models are available through the three national credit reporting agencies, which are Experian, Trans Union, and Equifax. All of the three models are often referred to as FICO scores. The scoring programs known at the three bureaus are: Beacon used for Equifax, Empirica used for Trans Union, and Fair Isaac Model used for Experian.

FICO scores range from approximately 375 to 900 points. Acceptable scores can vary according to the type of credit you are trying to obtain. Scores fall into three categories:

1. *650 or above.* You are considered the cream of the crop.
2. *620 to 650.* You are in a questionable category. This doesn't mean you won't be approved, but you will have to provide more documentation to the lender to satisfy its requirements.
3. *Below 620.* You may have to pay a higher interest rate.

FICO's scoring models are mathematical tables that assign points to different aspects of a consumer's profile and credit record. Fair Isaac uses credit data on millions of consumers, and applies mathematical modes to research credit patterns that will be used to predict how a consumer will perform in making their future payments.

When a credit report is run together as husband and wife by a credit grantor for purposes of qualifying for a line of credit, they will each have a FICO score; they are not viewed as one entity. Very seldom will both husband and wife have the same score. When qualifying jointly for a mortgage, the individual who has the highest income is the one whose score will count the most towards an approval.

FICO scores are top secret. Other than the companies who created the scoring system, no one seems to know how many points each factor is assigned. The score is based on all the credit-related information in the credit report. The five main areas that are reviewed for scoring are:

1. *Payment history.* Includes public records such as bankruptcies, judgments, and tax liens. Also included is derogatory information such as frequent delinquencies, collection accounts, late payments, and charged-off accounts that are noted in the trade line section of the credit report.

2. *Outstanding credit.* Includes the number of balances recently reported, the average balances, and the relationship between the total balances and total credit limits on revolving trade lines. You will be penalized if the balances are too close to their credit limit.

3. *Credit history.* Factors reviewed are the age of the oldest trade line, and the number of new trade lines. Trade lines that are within the past two years are given the most attention in the scoring.

4. *Pursuit of new credit.* The number of inquiries and new account openings in the last year are reviewed heavily. Recent inquiries are weighed heavily and used against you. Frequent inquiries will hurt your FICO score.

5. *Types of credit.* The number of trade lines reported for each type of credit such as: bankcards, travel and entertainment cards, department store cards, personal finance company loans, and installment loans.

A person who has a perfect credit report with no derogatory information can still receive a low FICO score by having too much debt.

There can be different FICO scores from each of three credit reporting agencies. To understand why a credit report scored the way it did, listed next to the score are four codes and underneath the codes are an explanation. These are the top four reasons, in order of severity, for the score.

It is important to know what your FICO score is; however the only way you could find your score out is by asking a credit grantor what the score is. You will not receive your score when you request your credit report from any of the three credit reporting agencies.

IMPROVING A LOW FICO SCORE

Q. *I turned in my application for a mortgage. I was told my FICO score was too low to get the best interest rates offered. Is there a way to improve my score and try to apply at a later date?*

Despite the fact that no one but Fair, Isaac, & Company know how the credit-scoring method works, there still seem to be some ideas on how to raise your FICO score.

- Review your past payment history on your credit report. Bankruptcies, foreclosures, collection accounts, and delinquencies will cost you big points. Contact the credit bureaus on any incorrect or inaccurate entries on your report. Do this before you apply for credit. Your payment record carries the most weight on your score.
- Scores are lower for consumers with no bank credit cards or those with five or more bank credit cards. Two to four cards are a good balance. If you decide to close any accounts, do not close your oldest accounts. The longer you have held an account, the better it is for your score.
- How much debt you carry on your credit cards and other accounts is the second biggest factor in determining your score. If your total debt is more than 75 percent of the total credit limits, your score will suffer. Keep your balances well below their credit limit.
- Avoid frequent inquiries. According to the score models, the risk of default appears to rise after two to four inquiries within six to twelve months. Inquiries are not picked up when consumers check their own credit report.
- Opening several new credit card accounts in a short period can hurt your score. If you have high balances on those new cards, your score will be lowered. Have one or two lines of new credit established within the past two years.
- More recent negative entries on your credit report are worse than problems that occurred years ago. An account that has been delinquent in the past six months will hurt you more than a bankruptcy five years ago. It appears that problems more than two years old won't hurt your score as much.
- Loans with finance companies will lower your credit score. Finance companies are companies who are a last resort to get cash and they charge extremely high interest rates.

If you are having problems paying your bills, prioritize them to avoid severe damage to your credit report. Pay your mortgage first, then your car payment, followed by payments on your credit cards and other revolving accounts. Don't make partial payments unless the credit grantor agrees to it and will not report the payments as late.

Once you have tried to raise your FICO score, wait four to six weeks before reapplying for your loan. It takes at least that long to have the creditors update your credit files. Have your loan officer run another credit report to see the results. If the FICO score is still too low, continue to find ways to improve it.

Don't allow several creditors to run inquiries on you unless you have first requested your credit report directly from the credit reporting agencies and made sure there were no problems that needed to be corrected first.

COST OF REFINANCING

Q. *We are thinking about refinancing our home to lower our interest rate. The cost of doing this seems outrageous. Is there a way to avoid all the costs of the refinance?*

Some banks and mortgage companies will advertise a no points/no fee loan. This type of loan may be appealing to save money with your closing costs, however nothing is ever free. The company will make its money by charging you a higher interest rate to absorb the cost of the loan and pay the fees for you.

As an incentive to get business, mortgage companies are paid a rebate from the lenders who offer loans. Usually the lower the interest rate, the higher the points. With a no fee loan, the interest rate will be higher, which will give a higher rebate to the mortgage company.

If you analyze both a no point/no fee loan, and a loan that offers a low interest rate and points, you may find in the long run it would be cheaper for you to pay the points and get the lower interest rate. The points and fees would be put into your loan.

If you plan on being in your home for three years or longer, a lower interest rate with points would be your best way to refinance. The cost of the loan will pay itself out over the three year period.

If you plan on selling your home within two to three years of refinancing it, the best way to set up your loan would be to pay the higher interest rate and not pay any points or fees. By doing this, you are not using the equity in your home for loan costs.

SUBPRIME LOANS

Q. *The past two years I have kept my credit report completely clean in order to overcome previous credit problems. I have built new credit with a car loan and an unsecured credit card. I have been told that if I purchase a home I still will have to make a large down payment and have to pay a high interest rate. Is this true?*

If you have had past credit problems, and they are more than two years old with new credit established and your FICO score is high enough, I would definitely try to qualify for a loan with lenders offering the best rates.

If you are having trouble being qualified for the lower rates due to a low FICO score, there are several subprime lenders who will give you a loan. I have helped individuals with bankruptcies more than two years old qualify for a new mortgage loan from a subprime lender with only a 5 percent down payment.

The best subprime loan for you is one that has a two year fixed interest rate that converts into an adjustable interest rate after 24 months. After the first two years, the interest rate increases. After 24 months of establishing a good mortgage history, you should refinance the loan with a company offering a lower fixed interest rate. Make sure the subprime loan does not have a prepayment penalty period longer than two years. You don't want to go past the two years with the subprime loan because the payment can go higher.

If you have had bad credit, the subprime loans are a good way to get a loan, even if you pay a higher interest rate. You can usually write off the interest on your taxes (check with your accountant), and by buying now, you are avoiding paying a higher price for your home later as prices continue to go up.

SHOPPING FOR A LOAN

Q. *We are purchasing our first home. Our credit is good. Should we shop around to different lenders to get the best interest rate? Once we are preapproved for the loan, should we lock in our interest rate?*

If you decide to shop around to different lenders, it is important that you let the first lender run a full credit report (called a standard factual) that lists your FICO scores. Make sure that you can get a copy of the credit report that lists the FICO score.

Use this full credit report to show to other lenders. You do not want the other lenders to run an additional credit report because the inquiries might lower your FICO score. There is enough information in the credit report for a lender to quote you an interest rate quote and list what charges you will entail.

I would suggest that you use a mortgage company to get your quotes. A mortgage company has access to many different lenders with competitive rates. A mortgage company also can shop for loans that will meet your needs. Because your credit is good, you won't have to worry about subprime loans. However, a mortgage company would have access to the traditional conventional, FHA, and VA loans, (as well as subprime lenders).

Once you have been preapproved for a loan and you have found the home you want to purchase, you can request to lock in your interest rate. The lock-in can range from 10 to 90 days. That means that the lock-in is only good up to the number of days you have locked it in for. If the loan approval runs over that time period, the lock-in will expire and you will have to renegotiate your interest rates.

It is not a good idea to lock in your loan until you have found your home and been preapproved for the loan. If the market interest rates are fluctuating, you might want to wait and see how low they will go. Locking an interest rate is almost like gambling because interest rates can move up or down daily.

RATIOS TOO HIGH

Q. *My husband and I are planning on buying our first home. We went to prequalify for a loan. Our income is good and our credit is excellent. The loan company said our ratios are too high to purchase a home in the price range we prefer. What does high debt ratios mean and can we reduce them?*

When you are being qualified for a mortgage, the lender wants to make sure that you can afford to make the payments. The lender will add up all your debts, plus the new proposed house payment (including principle, interest, taxes, insurance, and if applicable, a homeowner association monthly fee). (Installment loans that you are currently paying on will not count in qualifying if there are ten months or less left on the loan.) The lender will then divide this total by your gross monthly income. This will give the lender a ratio for qualification. Each loan program demands different qualification ratios. If yours is too high, ask your lender how high the ratio can be. Determine what debts you must pay off to get to the right ratio. You may need to consider purchasing a less expensive house to fit into the qualifying ratios that are required.

CHAPTER 7

UNDERSTANDING YOUR CREDIT REPORT

The Fair Credit Reporting Act gives the guidelines on what credit reporting agencies can and can't do regarding consumer's credit reports. The credit reporting agencies are regulated by the Federal Trade Commission (FTC). Any complaints you have against a credit reporting agency should be directed to the FTC.

Understanding your credit reports can be a problem. With three major credit reporting agencies holding information on more than 160 million Americans, errors can happen. The information that is stored in the credit bureaus is information that the creditors report to the bureaus.

Many individuals are afraid to see what is on their credit reports, but fear should never stop you from requesting your reports. Lack of knowledge on what is being reported about you can cause you embarrassment or shock when applying for credit. Even if you feel your credit is immaculate, be sure of what your credit report says about you.

Approximately 70 percent of the individuals who request credit reports will find some inaccuracies being reported. The key is understanding your credit report and knowing what you can do about problem entries.

Files are often crossed if you are a Sr., Jr., I, II, III, or if you have a common name such as John Smith.

Individuals have had accounts opened in their names without their knowledge. Credit fraud is not uncommon. All three of the credit reporting agencies, Experian (formerly TRW), Trans Union, and Equifax, have special programs on their computers that can show how many times your Social Security number and address has had inquiries. If it is in excess, someone may be trying to use your identification to get credit.

By requesting your credit report at least once a year (preferably every six months) from the three reporting agencies, you can know of any problems being reported and solve them before you request new credit.

Once you receive a copy of your credit report, review every entry, including your name, address, and Social Security number.

Understanding your credit report can be confusing. Experian (TRW) has made its reports easy for consumers to read. Each entry is numbered. A dash before and after the numbered entry indicates a negative entry.

Trans Union has put all the negative entries of your credit report on the first portion of your credit report. The negative entries have brackets (< >) around the creditors' names.

Equifax will code its entries for payment history by numbers 1 through 9. A number 1 is good; anything above that is negative. Carefully examine every entry to make sure it is correct.

You can receive your credit report from the following agencies:

Trans Union
P.O. Box 390
Springfield, PA 19064
800-888-4213

Equifax
P.O. Box 740193
Atlanta, GA 30374-0193
800-685-1111

Experian
P.O. Box 2104
Allen, TX 75013
888-EXPERIAN (888-397-3742)

Enclose $8 for each credit report. Include in your request your name, address, Social Security number, date of birth, and a photocopy of your driver's license or utility bill that has your name and address listed.

If you have been turned down for credit, you can request a free copy of your credit report within 60 days of being denied the credit. In your letter, give the name of the creditor who denied your credit application.

WHAT DOES SETTLED MEAN?

Q. *I paid off a bank loan for less than the amount owed. The bank agreed to this and listed my account as settled on my credit report. What does this mean? Would another credit grantor view this as a negative entry?*

Any time you pay off a debt for less than the amount due, the creditor will report to the credit bureau that the account was settled. The entry "settled" means that the account was paid off for less than the amount actually owed. This entry could be viewed as a negative entry by another creditor considering your application for credit. They would see that you did not pay your obligation according to the original terms of your contract.

When you are negotiating with a creditor and offering to settle your account for less than the amount due, make it part of the settlement that the creditor reports the account as paid in full to all credit bureaus. If it agrees to do this, get it in writing before you make the final payment. Trying to go back after you have paid the account and get the creditor to change the "settled" entry could be difficult.

THE CREDIT CARDS WERE PAID OFF

Q. *This year we are trying to get out of debt. We paid many of our accounts off and cut up the cards. They are still on our credit report. Why?*

Congratulations for trying to get out of debt. You must realize however that most of the creditors you have been paying are probably subscribers to Experian (TRW), Trans Union, and Equifax.

The Fair Credit Reporting Act allows credit entries—good or bad—to stay on your credit report for up to seven years from the last date of activity.

Negative entries would be slow paying account, delinquent accounts, charge-offs, collection accounts, judgments, tax liens, or foreclosures. Bankruptcies can remain on your credit report for up to ten years from the date they were filed or discharged.

When you cut up your credit cards, be sure to mail them back—certified mail with a return receipt—to the creditor with a letter cancelling your account. If you do not do this, the account will show that it is still active. Approximately three weeks after you send back your cut-up cards, request a copy of your credit reports to make sure the creditor has indicated that the account is closed.

UNAUTHORIZED INQUIRIES

Q. *There are inquiries listed on my credit report that I never authorized. Where did they come from?*

Anytime you apply for credit, the application you complete has in small print above your signature a statement authorizing the creditor to review your credit report and to exchange information about you with the credit reporting bureaus and other creditors. When you sign this application, you give the creditor authorization to make an inquiry to the credit reporting agencies about you and your paying habits.

When the inquiry is made by the creditor, the credit reporting agency must indicate on the credit report the date and name of the creditor making the inquiry. Any authorization for an inquiry to be made about you must be in writing.

Whenever you are shopping for credit for a car, bank loan, line of credit, etc., never give your name and Social Security number to just anyone. Many unscrupulous companies will run a credit report on you without your knowledge using just your name and Social Security number.

If you find inquiries made on your credit report that you never authorized in writing, contact the company that made the inquiry and request they remove it from your credit report. Ask the creditors where they got the authorization to run your report. If an authorization can't be verified, contact the credit reporting agency and demand that the information be removed.

Remember, however, the companies you have previously authorized and now have credit established with can make any number of inquiries on you at any time. They periodically will do this when reviewing your line of credit for a renewal.

CLOSED ACCOUNTS LISTED ON MY REPORT

Q. *There are accounts on my credit report that I never use. They are still being reported. I don't want them to be on my report. What can I do?*

A creditor can report your account whether good or bad to a credit reporting agency for up to seven years from the date of the last activity. Most people do not realize that once they have paid their credit card accounts off and do not intend to reuse the credit card, they must cut up the card and mail it back to the creditor with a letter indicating they want the account cancelled.

If the card is not sent back with a letter to cancel the account the creditor has no way of knowing that you do not intend to use the line of credit in the future.

Open lines of credit that may be on your credit report could hurt your chances of qualifying for new credit. Always cancel unused lines of credit unless you intend to use them in the future.

EMPLOYER CHECKING CREDIT REPORTS

Q. *My employer's name is on my credit report. Does that mean that my employer can check my credit report without my knowledge?*

An employer can't check your credit report unless you have signed an authorization. When applying for employment, many employment applications will have a statement indicating that the employer can verify your credit report.

Most people overlook the statement on the employment application authorizing the employer to verify their credit reports. With your signature on the application, the employer can do a background check about you which would consist of running your credit report.

Individuals working for insurance companies, banks, investment companies (such as stockbrokers), or any job where you would handle other people's money would require a background check. If an inquiry was made, you would see it on your credit report. It would show the date and company who ran the report.

Occasionally your current employer will periodically run your credit report to update its files.

PUBLIC NOTICES

Q. *My business failed and I had to file for bankruptcy. I had some judgments filed against me. Now everything is on my credit report. Why are these public notices on my credit report? How long does it take to come off?*

Any person can go to the county recorder's office and pick up information about an individual who has any document recorded in his or her name. This applies to judgments, bankruptcies, tax liens, mechanics' liens, and property owned. A judgment will be picked up by the credit reporting agencies from the county recorders office.

A judgment can remain on your credit report for up to seven years from the date it was entered by the court. A judgment is a public record and can also be picked up by a title company when you are trying to purchase, sell, or refinance your home. If you have sold your home or are refinancing, unless the judgments or liens were discharged through the bankruptcy, you will have to pay them off through escrow to deliver clear title.

If you have an unpaid judgment against you, most creditors will deny an approval of credit. The reason is that the party who has secured a judgment against you can secure it against your property, have your wages garnished, or levy your bank account to collect the amount owed.

Even if the judgment drops off your credit report prior to the seven years, it still remains in force. In some states, judgments expire after ten years; however, they can be renewed for an additional ten years. If the judgment is renewed, it should not be counted as a new negative on your credit report.

A bankruptcy is also a public notice and can remain on your credit report for up to ten years. It doesn't matter whether it is a Chapter 7 or Chapter 13 bankruptcy—the common personal bankruptcies. The ten years begins from the filing date of the bankruptcy.

Tax or mechanics' liens can remain on your credit report for up to seven years from the date recorded.

Any public notice not reported on your credit report still would show up if any type of background check was done on you. Just because a public notice is not mentioned in your credit report does not mean you don't owe it. When you pay off any type of lien or judgment, make sure it is recorded as paid or released so your record is current and correct.

CHARGE-OFF ACCOUNT

Q. *What does a "charge-off, profit and loss" mean on my credit report? Do I still have to pay the account off if it is written off?*

Usually a credit card account is charged off when the account becomes at least six months delinquent. The creditor has determined that there is no hope of collecting the money owed. A charge-off is an accounting practice for the creditor, but it will result in a negative credit item on your credit report.

Frequently, when an original creditor charges off an account, the creditor will hire a collection agency in an attempt to collect the debt.

If an account is charged off, the bank could come back and issue you a 1099-C tax form that would require you to report the debt as income. You would then be taxed on it unless you have filed for personal bankruptcy or can prove that you were insolvent when you stopped making your payments.

NEGATIVE ENTRIES

Q. *How long does negative information remain on a credit report?*

The Fair Credit Reporting Act allows a bankruptcy to remain on your credit report for up to ten years from the filing date. All other accounts—judgments, liens, charge-offs, slow pays, delinquent accounts, foreclosure and so on—can remain for up to seven years from the date of the last activity.

Many people get confused when reviewing their credit report. The confusion is between the date the credit was issued and the date of last activity. The date the credit was issued is irrelevant to removing the entry.

Removal is determined only by the date of the last activity or the last date a payment was received.

Good credit is treated the same way. If your account has been paid off and it has been seven years with no activity, the good account also will be deleted from your credit report. This is a frustration with people who have had past problems and the good credit is removed. Knowing how the system is set up enables you to keep a good record active and on your credit report.

PART

2

WORKING THROUGH CREDIT PROBLEMS

CHAPTER 8

CREDIT PROBLEMS

Nothing is more upsetting than facing credit and financial problems. Most individuals at some time in their life will experience financial hardship.

The problem is that when you start experiencing a financial problem, you have no clue how long it will last. Your optimistic side will say, "This is just temporary." But how temporary is anyone's guess. Like many people experiencing financial problems, you may begin robbing Peter to pay Paul. In other words, you start taking cash advances from your credit cards to pay other credit card bills as well as your living expenses. The intent is to pay everything back once you get back on your feet. The reality, however, is that you will be soon maxed out on your credit limits and not be able to pay anything. Your intention is good, but the outcome rarely turns out how you want it to.

Once you are maxed out on your credit cards and can't make any more payments, your creditors will begin calling and writing you letters wanting their payments. Your stress level will be at an all-time high. Most creditors are not very understanding. Their main concern is to update their computer files on your activity. Don't take their representatives' rude statements personally. They don't know you and they are only trying to do their jobs.

To avoid running out of money, the best thing to do before running up more debt is to make a plan on how you are going to survive. My book *The Insiders Guide to Managing Your Credit* (Dearborn, 1998) has extensive information on handling all credit and financial problems.

When creditors are threatening you with lawsuits and poor credit ratings, your first reaction is to pay them first. That is your first mistake of buckling under from their intimidation.

Too often I hear from people who pay the credit card bills just to silence the creditors. Then they run out of money to pay their utility or housing expenses. The result may be their electricity, gas, and phone may be turned off. Or they may even become homeless.

Remember, when you are going through financial and credit problems and making your payments late, your credit report is already ruined. There isn't a whole lot more that the creditors can do except sue you. It would be hard for the creditor to collect any money from you through a lawsuit if you have no money or assets. That is why lawsuits are not that common. Most of the time the creditor will just charge off your account—write it off their books as a loss.

Having a plan before you run out of money will enable you to make your money last longer. It will give you a chance to come up with a long-term solution rather than running around putting out fires.

ERIC'S STORY

Eric attended one of my seminars and afterwards stayed to discuss his situation. He said, "My income has dropped by 30 percent. I have fallen behind in making my house payment and credit card payments. The bill collectors are calling and writing to me demanding payments. I feel like I am paralyzed. I don't know who to pay first. When I pay the credit cards, I can't pay my house payment. I feel so out-of-control with this situation. It seems whoever is yelling the loudest is the company I pay first. How do I determine who to pay first?"

Eric was so stressed out that he was having trouble sleeping. His work was suffering because his mind would only stay focused on his financial problems.

The first thing I told Eric to do was to make a list of all his bills and expenses. This list needed to include the rent or mortgage payment, utilities, credit card and installment payments, food, transportation, and any other payments or miscellaneous items.

Once the list was complete, I had Eric separate his survival payments—food, house payment, utilities, and medical costs. These are essentials and must always be paid first. The remaining items on his list should once again be prioritized. Next may be a car payment, gasoline, and mandatory car insurance if he needs to drive to work.

The remaining bills would be credit card and installment loans. These are considered nonessential and should be paid only after the essential bills are paid. If there was not enough money to pay everything, I instructed Eric to call the creditors and make special arrangements. I told Eric, "If there is not enough money left to pay the nonessentials bills, then pay them when you can. Be prepared for constant telephone calls and letters demanding payment, but stay firm and focused on paying your essential bills."

Once Eric made this plan of attack, he was able to focus on the solution of making more money rather than drowning in stress.

Eric was able to pick up a part-time job to supplement his regular income and get back on track paying his bills.

AUTO REPOSSESSION

Q. *I was three weeks late in making my car payment. The bank repossessed my car. They are demanding $2,500 from me to get my car back. I don't have the money. What happens if they keep the car?*

One of the first things you want to do is ask the bank to reinstate your loan contract. See if the bank will add the past due payment plus costs that resulted from the repossession onto your loan. If the bank agrees to this arrangement, you will not have to repay the balance in full immediately.

Most lenders do not repossess cars until at least two payments are missed. Legally the lender can take action when a payment is only one day late or if the lender feels there is reason to believe the borrower is unable to keep making regular payments. If your payments are consistently late, the lender will not have much tolerance and could deem that reason enough to repossess the car quicker than if you show an occasional late payment.

If the bank won't rewrite your contract and is still demanding the full amount, the bank could sell the car at an auction to raise money to satisfy the debt. Usually at the sale the car is sold for less than the amount due on the loan. The amount remaining is called a "deficiency," which you will be required to pay. If you don't pay it, the bank can go to court and get a judgment against you.

Your credit report will reflect the repossession as well as any amount that is still owed on the account after the sale of the car. Having a repossession on your credit report will make it difficult to get another auto loan.

If you can resolve the repossession by getting the car returned, you might try to refinance the car for a longer term to get lower monthly payments.

BREACH OF CONTRACT

Q. *I signed a two-year contract with a fitness gym. The contract was set up to deduct the monthly dues automatically from my checking account. Six months before my contract expired with the gym, I closed my checking account. I never heard from the gym regarding any further payments. I recently got my credit report and discovered the gym had turned my account over to a collection agency. I want to settle this. If I pay this off in full, will the collection agency remove this from my credit report?*

There is always a catch when getting a membership at a gym. I have seen many credit reports with collection accounts from gyms. Most people don't read the fine print when joining a gym and end up paying for longer terms than they realized or being charged extra fees to cancel their memberships before the end of their contracts.

First I would recommend that you contact the gym and see if you can pay them directly. If they agree, have the gym contact the collection agency to delete the entry. Get everything in writing from the gym before you settle the account.

If the gym won't work with you, contact the collection agency and see how much they will accept to settle the account. Ask the collection agency for a letter stating what they will accept and that the collection agency will agree to remove the entry from your credit report. The collection agency is under no obligation to remove this account or settle for anything less than what is owed.

If the collection agency will not cooperate with you, the Fair Credit Reporting Act will allow you to put a statement on your credit report explaining your side of the story.

EVERY MONTH GOING FURTHER IN THE HOLE

Q. *My bills are out of control. Every month I am going further in the hole. I have fallen behind on some credit card payments. I don't own a home so I can't get a home equity loan. I have heard of some debt consolidation companies who can help me. Is it better to go through a debt consolidation company or try and negotiate on my own?*

Remember one thing. Your credit report is already damaged. Without owning a home it is difficult to get any cash from an unsecured loan.

A debt consolidation company who would work with you could set up payments between you and the creditors. Some debt consolidation companies are nonprofit while others will make a profit. Nothing is free. There is always a way the companies will make money.

If you are set up making payments to the debt consolidation company, you are probably making interest payments with each payment to the company. Some of the nonprofit companies have special arrangements with the creditors where the creditors will pay the company a percentage of the debt. Either way the companies are being paid with your money.

If you decide to negotiate payments directly with the creditors you will be saving any cost that you would be paying the debt consolidation company. You would not be creating a larger bill. Make sure you can keep up the payment arrangements you make with the creditors and not fall behind.

Always prioritize your bills on which ones to pay first. Refer to Eric's story at the beginning of the chapter.

FORECLOSURE PROCEEDINGS

Q. *I am three months late on my mortgage. I have been in contact with the bank to try and work things out. They said that they were going to start foreclosure proceedings against me. How long does that give me to raise the money I need to bring everything current. Can they throw me in the streets?*

The first thing the bank will do to begin foreclosure proceedings is to file a "Notice of Default" letter requesting all the back payments plus foreclosure costs. This is mailed by certified mail with a return receipt that will have your signature on it.

The notice of default will give you 90 days to bring all the payments current. If you don't bring the payments current within the 90 days, the lender will set a date for a public sale of your property, which usually occurs approximately 30 days from the date of the first publishing of the sale. The published notice of the sale will list the address of the house, information about the loan, and the time and location of the sale. Some lenders will allow you to reinstate the loan before the sale: others may require a total payoff of the loan balance. Every state has its own policies.

At the end of the sale you must vacate the property; it no longer belongs to you.

The total process of the foreclosure is approximately 120 days from the date of the notice of default.

AVOIDING FORECLOSURE

Q.   *Three years ago we refinanced our home. The market fell and now the loan is higher than the appraised market value. We are having problems keeping up our payments. We are trying to avoid a foreclosure. What will a foreclosure do to our credit rating?*

A foreclosure on your credit report will hurt your chances of getting into another property. Most lenders are afraid to take a risk with someone who has had a foreclosure. Some subprime lenders will entertain the application only if the foreclosure is at least two years old.

There are three ways that you can fight a foreclosure.

1. Many lenders will consider a "hardship application" that would describe a borrower's problem and be viewed as a temporary situation. If you can prove to the lender that the situation you are in is only temporary, many times it will work with you in setting up a repayment plan.

   Possible solutions would be to change your loan terms such as lowering your interest rate, extending the loan period, or refinancing.

2. To avoid ruining your credit report, get the lender to agree to a short sale. If the lender sees that you can't make the payments and the property value is less than your outstanding loan amount, it may agree to let someone purchase your property for less than the loan balance.

   The only way a lender will entertain a short sale is to review your financial hardship. Most lenders won't talk to you about a short sale if you are current on your payments and show no struggle. If you fall behind in your payments, then they will talk to you about your situation. The lender does not want your property. The cost of a foreclosure is costly and time consuming. The lender just wants to be paid. If it means taking a loss on the loan by a short sale and it is in its best interest, the lender will do it. You will then be released from the liability of the loan.

   There are times that lenders will allow you to quit claim deed the property to the lender. That means you are deeding the property and title to the lender in exchange for closing the loan. This will avoid a foreclosure.

3. Bankruptcy is another option to stall a foreclosure. You should seek the advice of an attorney or accountant who can direct you and explain what your options may be should you seek bankruptcy.

TAX LIEN ON MY CREDIT REPORT

Q. *I keep getting letters from the Internal Revenue Service demanding payment for an old tax bill. I don't have the money to pay them. The IRS put a tax lien against me and now it shows up on my credit report. What can I do about this? I keep getting turned down for credit because of the tax lien.*

Whenever you fall delinquent on paying your taxes, if you have not set up some type of repayment arrangement the IRS will put a tax lien against you.

A tax lien is filed and recorded with the county clerk's office. It then becomes a public record.

The credit reporting agencies will pick up the tax lien after it is recorded and list it on your credit report. Unless the tax lien is paid off this will be viewed as negative whenever you are applying for credit. This unpaid tax lien also will need to be paid off if you are trying to purchase a home, refinance your home, or sell your home. If you are selling, purchasing, or buying property, the tax lien could be paid off through your escrow.

I would suggest that you contact the IRS and make payment arrangements. The IRS will require a financial statement from you to determine what payments you can afford. Discuss with the IRS the possibility of removing the tax lien once you are set up with a payment schedule.

If you are trying to get new credit, unless the lien is removed or paid off it will be difficult. If you are applying for a car loan, many times the lender will overlook the tax lien if you can show them a written agreement from the IRS regarding payment.

If you are trying to refinance your home and you have an unpaid tax lien, contact the IRS and see if they will subordinate the lien. If the IRS agrees to this, you can complete your refinance.

TAKING ME TO COURT

Q. *A year ago I fell behind in making my payments. One of the credit card companies that I never paid just served me court papers for a lawsuit. How can I solve this without going to court?*

If you don't respond to the papers you were served with within 30 days of receipt, you will automatically lose the case by default.

To settle this without going to court, contact the lender who filed the lawsuit. Offer to pay the lender whatever you can afford. Many times the lenders will settle for a less amount just to get your account off their books. If the lender agrees to settle the account with you prior to the court date, have the lender issue you a letter that they are withdrawing the lawsuit, and to indicate the terms of your agreement in the letter.

Lawsuits are costly and most lenders don't want to pursue this form of collection. If the lender does get a judgment against you, it will appear on your credit report and hurt your chances of obtaining new credit.

MAKING LESS THAN THE MINIMUM PAYMENT

Q. *I am having trouble making my payments. Instead of sending the minimum payment on my credit cards I have been sending at least $10 per month for the past three months. I figured something was better than nothing. Now the creditors are screaming that I am behind and threatening to turn me over to a collection agency. What is their problem? I have been paying them something.*

Always call the creditor first to find out if they will accept less than the minimum payment.

The problem with sending less than the minimum payment is that the difference between the amount you are sending and the payment required still leaves an unpaid payment.

What is happening is that the unpaid payment that is remaining is rolled into the next billing cycle. This will continue to happen every month that your minimum payment is not covered. It reflects as a late payment. It is called a rolling late payment because it rolls into the following month.

Because this has been going on for the past three months the creditor's computer is signaling three months' delinquency. Until you pay the whole payment required this will continue and the creditor will take steps to turn your account over to a collection agency.

I would suggest that you contact the creditor, explain your situation, and see if you can work out a reduced payment schedule, including no added late fees, until your finances are freed up. Until you do that your account and credit report will reflect a delinquency.

CHAPTER 9

DEATH, DIVORCE, AND MARITAL PROBLEMS

It is amazing at the trauma that results when married couples don't communicate about their finances. It seems that with most couples, one is a spender and the other is a saver. One spouse controls the finances, the other spouse has no clue as to what their financial situation really is.

It's no wonder that finances is one of the top three reasons for marital problems and divorces. If it doesn't cause divorce, it will cause stress, anxiety, arguments, and communication problems. Secrets in the marriage regarding finances always manage to come out.

My friend Tina's husband was murdered. They had their own business. When things had settled down, she discovered that he had several bank accounts and credit cards that she was not aware of. Every day was a new discovery. Tina had to take the business over and try to run it, not knowing what accounts were outstanding. Had her husband shared with her their financial situation, whereabouts of his bank accounts, what debts he had incurred, and other pertinent financial information prior to his death, Tina would have had an easier time making things run smoother.

With divorces at a record high, most couples don't discuss openly what their financial situation is and who is to take responsibility for paying the bills after the divorce is final. Without properly notifying the creditors of the divorce and cancelling open joint credit cards, both spouses are liable for the debts. Creditors must be notified and must authorize any agreement drawn to release and remove the spouse who will not be responsible for the payment.

Problems with credit cards after divorce can come back to haunt you if you don't take the proper steps to release yourself from the liability.

JAN'S STORY

Jan and Tom were married exactly one year to the day when Tom suddenly became ill and died. Jan was devastated. Tom was 42 years old and Jan was 36 years old when they were married. This was the first marriage for both. Tom had a small life insurance policy, but not enough for Jan to live on after the burial.

Prior to the marriage, Tom had $36,000 in credit card debt. Jan had $5,000 of credit card debt going into the marriage.

After Tom's death, Jan notified all of Tom's creditors of his death. The creditors told Jan that she was responsible for the debts and they must be paid. Many of the creditors began calling and writing letters to Jan demanding payment. It wasn't enough that Jan was grieving the loss of her husband, but now she had to contend with creditors seeking payment for bills she never incurred.

When Jan told me her situation, I advised her to see an attorney. After counsel, she was told that she only owed money on whatever debts she and Tom incurred after they were married. The debts prior to their marriage were not hers. Letters were sent by the attorney to all of Tom's creditors, who stopped contacting her.

The problem with many creditors and collection agencies is that they will try to bully innocent people who don't know their rights into paying bills they don't owe. This is done to get their accounts off their books. The wise thing to do after the death of a spouse is to contact an attorney and find out what your rights are. This will give you wisdom when trying to handle situations such as Jan's.

MARTIN AND LINDA'S STORY

Linda frantically called my office. She asked me if I could help her get a consolidation loan without her husband's knowledge. As she was talking to me, she stopped suddenly and said, "I'll call you back, Martin just got home and I have to think of a way to tell him I have ruined his credit." As she hung the telephone up I could only imagine the scene that was to take place.

Martin called me the next day to say his wife had told him she had secretly run up $25,000 in credit card debt. He thought that she had been making the monthly payments, only to find out she had not. The bill collectors were calling and his credit was ruined.

The house was in Martin's name, so I suggested that we try to get a new second trust deed on his home to pay back the bills. I told him to contact all the creditors and explain his situation, to ask if they would discount the amount he owed if he paid them off. Almost all the creditors agreed. I helped Martin to get a new second trust deed loan using the equity in his home. All the bills were then paid off.

During the time that Martin and I were trying to get his loan and he was negotiating with his creditors to discount the balances, Linda had called me. She told me that she was frustrated with her marriage, and angry with Martin. She felt the only way to get back at him was to run up the credit card balances and then try to ruin his credit. Her plan got out of hand, because she didn't realize the backlash from the harassment from the creditors.

The day she confessed to Martin what she had done was a turning point in their marriage. Martin realized that he had not taken the time to communicate with Linda about their finances and that it was important for both of them to be involved. Instead of ruining their marriage, the confession strengthened it with regard to communicating on issues that had been swept under the table.

I wouldn't recommend this extreme situation to solve a marital problem because it could turn out the other way. Open communication and awareness of your finances is a must for a marriage to survive any financial situation.

RUINED CREDIT AFTER DIVORCE

Q.   *I recently divorced. My husband has ruined my credit. I'm scared to see what my credit report says about me. What can I do?*

First, don't panic! Not seeing your credit report prevents you from deleting any inaccuracies that are being reported.

Many times a wife will have less information on her report than the husband because she was not the originator of the line of credit, or the line of credit is only in the husband's name.

Your report may not be as bad as you think. Request credit reports from all three credit reporting bureaus. Review each report and dispute with the credit reporting agency any incorrect, inaccurate, or erroneous information that appears on it. The credit reporting agency must investigate your dispute with the creditor and remove any items that are not correct or verifiable by the creditor.

If there is debt information on your credit report that is your husband's responsibility to pay, contact the credit reporting agency and direct them to notify the creditor.

HE AGREED TO MAKE PAYMENTS BUT DIDN'T

Q. *My divorce decree says my ex-husband was to make the payments on the credit cards that we held jointly. He quit making the payments and now the creditors are coming after me and my credit report is ruined? What can I do?*

Unfortunately most couples who divorce have the misconception that they are released from any credit obligation for payments if the judge orders either the husband or wife to be solely responsible for making a specific payment.

When you apply for credit jointly, you both are responsible for the repayment of the debt. If your husband was ordered to make the payments on the debt owed and he doesn't, the creditors legally can pursue you for payment. The creditor will continue to report all payment history on both of you as long as the account is open and is held jointly.

Contact the creditor and explain your situation. Ask the creditor to release you from the liability of this debt and remove your name from the account. Your ex-husband must be in agreement with this and should support this agreement with a letter to the creditor. Your ex-husband must state in his letter that he will take full responsibility for the payments.

Should the creditor agree to do this, you will no longer be responsible for the account. Your name will be removed from the account. All payment and credit history on that account will stop being reported on your credit report.

USE YOUR WIFE'S GOOD CREDIT TO PURCHASE A HOME

Q. *I was divorced and recently remarried. My credit is in terrible shape but my wife's is excellent. We want to purchase a home. We both have good paying jobs. Will my bad credit pull her down?*

Yes! You need to be very careful when you are applying for any new credit, whether it be for a credit card or a mortgage. The way the credit system works is that when you are applying for new credit jointly, your negative credit will not be strong enough to qualify even with your wife's excellent credit. This is especially true if your income is higher than your wife's.

A credit grantor will look at the wage earner who is making the highest salary to determine an approval or denial. If your income is higher than your wife's, the credit grantor will evaluate the application on your creditworthiness rather than your wife's.

The best thing to do is to have your wife apply for new credit. Once she has been approved, she can request another credit card for you with your name on it. She can request the card to be a joint or user card. She will be responsible for making the payments. This will help you add new credit to your credit report.

If you are applying for a mortgage, wait until the new credit is seasoned for at least a year. I would suggest that your wife apply in her name only. If she is approved for the mortgage, she will be the one solely responsible for the payments. Her name will be the one recorded on the title. After the loan is closed, your wife can file a quit claim deed adding you to the title. It must be recorded with the county recorder's office.

After you have reestablished your credit history you can refinance your home jointly.

CHARGES MADE AFTER DIVORCE

Q. *After my divorce I discovered my ex-wife was still using the charge cards that we had together. Can she do this?*

Unless you specifically addressed the disbursements of your credit card accounts in your divorce, your wife can still use the credit cards. Obviously this is the wrong thing to do because you are still jointly responsible for making the payments, no matter who made the new purchase.

It is important to know which of you is the primary person responsible for the account. You can call the credit card company to find out if you or your wife were the primary applicants. You also can check your credit reports to see which of the accounts listed reflect the accounts as joint, individual, or a user card. If your accounts were taken out in your wife's name and you are a user of the account, contact the creditor and request that it removes your name from the account. If the account is a joint account, you need to notify the credit card company immediately requesting your name be removed from the account and stating that you have no liability for any activity since the divorce. If you were the primary applicant for the credit card, you can request in writing that the account be closed. This would stop new activity on the account. Your wife should agree to make the payments because they are for her purchases; however if she doesn't, you still can be held liable for payment because you were the primary applicant. Remember, unless you resolve these problems with your ex-wife and take the appropriate action, the activity will continue to be reported on your credit report.

IRS PROBLEMS AFTER MY DIVORCE

Q. *I was divorced four years ago. The divorce was messy. My husband ruined my credit. Now the Internal Revenue Service is after me to collect taxes they say I owe. I'm terrified! I'm scared to see my credit report. What can I do?*

Rather than be afraid to see your credit report, you need to face whatever problems you are having and resolve them. Fear is felt when you don't know what you are facing. By jumping in and facing your fears, you can make a plan and the solutions will then be clearer.

First, request a copy of your credit report from all three credit reporting agencies. Check to see if the IRS has filed any tax liens against you. Review any items on your credit report that are not accurate or not yours. Dispute each item on your credit report that is not accurate or is not yours by writing a letter to the credit reporting agencies.

If the money the IRS is indicating that you owe was from the years that you were married to your husband and they can't collect from your ex-husband, they will try to collect from you. If you are in financial hardship, you can complete a financial statement showing the hardship. The IRS may allow you to make small payments or if the hardship is great enough they will put you in an uncollectible status.

If the money the IRS is trying to collect from you is for taxes owed by your ex-husband after your divorce, I would suggest you see a tax attorney. You are not responsible for taxes from returns after your divorce that were not filed jointly.

LACK OF CONTROL

Q. *My husband and I have separate credit card accounts. He refuses to discuss our finances. I discovered that he has overextended his credit and fallen behind in making his payments. Will I be affected by his lack of self-control when it comes to paying his bills?*

The worse thing to do in a marriage is to keep secrets—especially when it comes to money. It is important for spouses to keep each other informed on all financial matters. Should your spouse die and you were not aware of the condition of your finances prior to your spouse's death, tremendous pressure and problems could result from this lack of communication. The bills are still due and payable, even with the death of a spouse.

You need to know what credit card debts each of you have, what life insurance your spouse has, and the location of the policy. You also need to know of any bank accounts, retirement funds, and stocks, bonds, and other investments. Without this information, you could feel like you are destitute.

Many times the person who is the compulsive spender will try to hide credit card purchases and loans. If the spending gets so out of control that debts are too high and can't be paid, that's usually when the confession comes.

In a community property state, both husband and wife are responsible for repayment of the debts. Credit cards and loans that are in your husband's name alone will affect only his credit rating. Only if your name is listed on any debts can the credit card companies report the payment history on your credit report.

Write a plan for repayment that both you and your husband can live with. Consolidating the credit card debt into one credit card may be an option. That would mean transferring balances from one credit card to another lower interest credit card. If you own a home, you could consider taking out a consolidation loan to pay the credit card companies.

However you decide to repay his debts, I would suggest that you each limit yourself to one credit card each. Close all other open credit card accounts: This would eliminate the temptation of using them. Pay cash whenever possible and pay the credit card balances off every month. If that isn't a possibility, pay as much as you can—not just the minimum due. Keeping outstanding balances low will lower the amount you'll pay in interest.

CHAPTER 10

CREDIT CARD AND CHARGE CARD PROBLEMS

When you have been approved for a credit or charge card, you are responsible for the purchases made with the credit card and the payment for such purchases.

If you have other authorized users of your credit card making purchases, you are still responsible for the payment. The person who is the originator of the credit card application is the person from whom the credit card company will seek to collect payments. The originator of the card also is the one whose credit report will reflect information on balances and payment history.

Several problems can arise with having charge cards. If a card is lost or stolen but not reported to the creditor, you can be liable for unauthorized purchases. Keep a list of all your credit and charge cards, including the name, address, and telephone number of each company; and your account number. Keep the list in a safe place. If your credit cards are ever lost or stolen, you will be able to contact the customer service department immediately to cancel the credit cards.

If your credit card has been lost or stolen, the credit card company will issue a new card with a different account number. The only reason a credit card company won't issue a new card is if you have had previous problems paying the account.

Unauthorized charges are another problem that could arise with credit cards. Credit card fraud is on the rise across the country. It is important that you safeguard your credit card and credit card account numbers.

When you use your credit card for purchases, always keep your sales receipt. Frequently the merchant will input your credit card number into its system and it prints out on the receipt. If your account number gets into the wrong hands from information on a receipt, there could easily be unauthorized purchases made. The time it takes to keep proper track of your receipts is tiny compared to the time it will take trying to convince the charge company you *didn't* make a purchase.

The Fair Credit Billing Act gives you the right to withhold your payment to the credit card company for defective merchandise or inferior service, *if* certain conditions are met. If you withhold your payment, only withhold the amount for the item in dispute. If you have other purchases included in the statement that you are disputing you must pay for the purchases not include in your dispute. If payment is withheld, the credit card company cannot put any derogatory information on your credit report and cannot report the account as delinquent while the charge is disputed.

Billing errors do occur. Review your statement every month to make sure there are no unauthorized purchases. Credit and charge card billing errors are governed by the Fair Credit Billing Act. An explanation of your billing rights and finance charges is located on the back of your statement. If you discover an error in your statement, you must immediately write a letter to the card issuer.

During the time that you are disputing your bill, the creditor cannot report your account delinquent to any credit reporting agency and cannot pursue collection activity on the disputed amount until it is resolved. To protect your credit rating, be sure to pay the amount owed to the creditor for items that are not being disputed. The only amount that can be withheld from the payment is the disputed amount.

TIFFANY AND MIKE'S STORY

Tiffany and Mike moved to a new home and had all their mail forwarded to the new address. Tiffany notified all their creditors of their new mailing address, but one of the creditors never received her correspondence listing the change.

Several weeks later the credit card company called Tiffany to confirm an order for some toys. It appeared that the billing address didn't match the mailing address that was given for a purchase. Also the telephone number given didn't match the telephone number the credit card company had on record.

Tiffany indicated that she had not placed an order for any toys. The credit card company gave Tiffany the name of the toy company that received the order, and the address and telephone of the person who indicated she was Tiffany.

First Tiffany telephoned the store where the order was placed. The woman at the store who took the order indicated that she had just spoken to the person who had placed the order. Tiffany explained that she never placed the order and to cancel it. She then made a telephone call to the number that was given her.

A woman answered the telephone and Tiffany said, "Hello, is this Tiffany? I'm calling to confirm your order for the toys you just ordered to be shipped to this address."

The womans response was, "Yes, I'm Tiffany and the address is correct."

Tiffany was infuriated with this woman and responded, "You're not Tiffany, I am, and lady you're in big trouble."

The woman hung up. Tiffany immediately called the sheriff, who went to the address that had been given. It turned out to be a hotel, and the woman had just checked out.

The credit card company did not charge or process the order. However, if the company had not called Tiffany to confirm the mailing address and telephone number, credit card fraud would have occurred.

It is not uncommon to hear of people stealing credit card statements from mailboxes. Your name, address, and account number is recorded on the statement. It's enough information for an unscrupulous individual to make purchases with companies who don't have a tight security system for the credit card orders.

DAMAGED PRODUCT

Q. *I received a damaged product from a mail order company. The purchase was made on my credit card. I disputed the amount, but the mail order company still got the money. The credit card company is now reporting my account as a R9 charge-off. The creditors will not cooperate in removing it from my credit report. Help!*

When you receive a damaged product, you should immediately telephone the company. Keep a record of the date and time you phoned and with whom you spoke. Get a return authorization number, if that company uses them. Then return the product to the mail order company along with a letter stating the problem. Request a return receipt from your shipper so you can prove the item made it back to the seller. Most reputable companies will replace the damaged product with a new one.

If the company refuses to replace the damaged item, make a written complaint to the company on whose card you charged the item. (Send this dispute letter certified mail with a return receipt.)

You have a right to refuse payment of the item if the credit card company is notified within 60 days from the date the credit card statement was mailed. The credit card company has 30 days to acknowledge receipt of your letter. At this point, the creditor will make the necessary corrections on your account and notify you in writing of the correction or a written explanation of why you are incorrect.

During the time you are disputing your account, you are not required to pay that portion of the bill which you are disputing. The credit card company cannot report you as delinquent on that portion of the bill. It is important to remember when you are disputing a purchase to pay the credit card company what is owed on your other purchases. If you stop paying on your account you risk a poor credit rating.

If you refuse to pay on your account, and did not follow the procedure listed above to dispute the purchase with the mail order company and credit card company, after several months of receiving no payment the credit card company would charge off your account. This would be entered on your credit report.

The best thing for you to do is contact your credit card company and ask them to settle your account. Offer to pay them less than they are requesting in exchange for the entry to be removed entirely from your credit report, or to reflect a paid in full status. You have nothing to lose by making such an offer. If the entry is accurate on your credit report, it can remain on your credit report for seven years.

STOLEN IDENTITY

Q. *I received a copy of my credit report and discovered there were several open credit accounts that are not mine. It appears that someone is using my name and Social Security number to open these accounts. What can I do?*

It is important to safeguard any documentation that has your name and Social Security number listed. With that information another person can fraudulently open credit card accounts without your knowledge. They get away with it by using a different mailing address for the statement.

Many people have been taken advantage of by someone stealing their identification. Because the information given on the credit application has your name and Social Security number, an account can be opened and reported to the credit reporting agencies. An individual who has stolen your identity can damage your credit report by not making payments on the accounts that were opened. You would never know this was happening unless you received a copy of your credit report.

To clear this up, contact the credit card company listed on the credit report. The account number on the credit report must be included on any correspondence you send to the creditor.

Most companies have a special customer service department for fraudulent accounts. Explain the situation, mentioning that you never authorized or completed an application for this account. Ask to see a copy of the application that they have on file. The person signing the application will have a different signature from yours.

The credit card company must initiate an investigation. You are not responsible for the charges as long as the company cannot prove the person who initiated and signed the application was you. Criminal charges can be pressed against the person who fraudulently opened this account.

All correspondence you have with the credit card company during this investigation should be mailed certified mail with a return receipt. If you telephone the credit card company, make sure you get the names of any individuals with whom you speak. Keep detailed notes of the date, time, person you spoke with, and what was discussed during the conversation.

Once you have resolved the matter with the credit card company, make sure you get their statement on their letterhead indicating that this is not your account. Insist that they contact all credit reporting agencies, deleting the information. Follow up with a letter requesting removal of the item, with a copy of the letter from the creditor to all three credit reporting agencies. Mail this certified mail with a return receipt. You should get an updated credit report from the credit reporting agencies within 45 days showing they have deleted the item.

LOST WALLET

Q.   *I lost my wallet and someone started making purchases with my VISA card. Am I responsible?*

When you discover that your wallet is lost, the first thing you need to do is immediately contact every credit card company that you have an account with and cancel your cards.

Federal law limits your liability for unauthorized charges made on your credit cards. You must notify the card issuer within a reasonable time, generally within 30 days. You are not responsible for any charges made after the notification. Your personal liability is limited to $50 for charges made prior to notification of the card. Any delay in reporting the loss will cause you to be liable for all charges made on the credit card before the time of notification.

Many credit card companies are imprinting your photo on the credit cards. This is for your protection should your card be lost or stolen. Also you want to always sign the back of all your credit cards. Your signature should then be matched by a merchant whenever you make any purchases. This also is for your protection.

MULTIPLE CHARGES

Q.   *I received my credit card statement with multiple charges from a hotel that I stayed at. I paid the bill with my credit card but the statement had other charges from the hotel on it that I never authorized. What can I do?*

The first thing you want to do is call the credit card company to see who made the charges and if they were referenced by the hotel.

Then call the hotel with the information that you have and ask them to verify the charges. Many times when a reservation is made and you check in at a hotel, the hotel will put a hold on your credit card for the amount of days you will be staying. If the amount they are trying to hold is too large and the credit card company does not accept the hold, the hotel will try using smaller increments of funds. For example, if the estimated bill is $200 and your credit card won't accept $200, the hotel will try to put $50 increments onto the card to total the $200.

Frequently, when you go to check out, the hold on your credit card is not lifted for several days. Therefore, what appears on your statement is the small increment charges that were used to hold your account, plus the charges you actually made while staying at the hotel.

If you discover that the hotel has not released the hold on your credit card, instruct the hotel to contact your credit card company immediately and initiate the release of the hold. This should credit your account with the amount of money that was placed on hold.

Contact the credit card company within five days of your call from the hotel to verify that the hold was withdrawn. If it has not been withdrawn, send a letter to the credit card company and hotel refusing to pay for the charge.

BILLING ERRORS

Q. *I received my American Express credit card statement and noticed a charge at a hotel I never stayed at. I contacted American Express and they indicated they would check into it. How long does that take?*

It is important that you always review your credit card statements to make sure there are no errors on it. Many people get their monthly statement and never look at the charges on it.

Don't assume that your complaint will be handled by a mere telephone call. It is important that you write American Express a letter indicating the billing error. The letter must be sent within 60 days from the date the statement was mailed (check the postmark). This letter should be sent certified mail with a return receipt.

According to the Fair Credit Billing Act, if a complaint of a billing error is mailed to an institution, the institution has 30 days to acknowledge receipt of your letter. During that time period the creditor will make the necessary corrections on your account and notify you in writing of the correction. If the creditor discovers that there was no error, it must send you a written explanation of why you are incorrect. If the creditor indicates that you are incorrect, it must provide you with documentation to support its findings.

During the time that you are disputing the bill, the creditor cannot report your account delinquent to any credit reporting agency and cannot pursue collection activity on the disputed amount. A dispute with the creditor regarding an error must not take any longer to settle than two billing cycles or a 90-day period, whichever is longer.

MY FATHER'S STORY

Several years ago I was visiting my father. He took me out to dinner to a well-respected restaurant in Hollywood, paying for dinner with a credit card.

Two weeks after our dinner together he received a telephone call from the credit card company that he charged the restaurant bill to. The company indicated that there had been multiple purchases made on his credit card and they wanted to confirm that he was the one making these charges. After reviewing the charges that were made, it was discovered that someone had been making these purchases without my father's knowledge.

As we retraced the purchases, it appeared that when he had charged our dinner, he was given a carbon copy that he didn't destroy. The carbon copy was tossed into the restaurant's trash and someone had retrieved it. The numbers on the carbon copy was his account number with his name and signature.

This made dad an easy target for credit card fraud. The person who had stolen the carbon copy was using the account number to make purchases.

Once this was discovered, the credit card company canceled the card and issued dad a new one. The credit card company did not charge him for the purchases, but it was a valuable lesson for all of us. Never leave receipts or their carbons lying around. You never know who may get ahold of your account number.

TIPS TO AVOID CREDIT CARD FRAUD

1. Always destroy your carbon copies.
2. Keep all receipts with your credit card numbers in a safe place or destroy them.
3. Never give out your name, address, or Social Security number to anyone on the telephone or in person unless you know what they will be doing with the information.
4. If you move, always contact your creditors immediately with your new address and have all your mail forwarded.
5. Never put your bills with checks in a mailbox that is easily accessible to the public. Someone can steal it from your mailbox and gain access to your account numbers.

CHAPTER 11

PROBLEMS FROM COSIGNING FOR A LOAN

Most of us have no understanding of the risk we take when we cosign for a loan. We all have a difficult time saying "no," to our children, relatives, or even friends when asked for help. So when we agree to cosign for a loan, we don't contemplate the problems that can arise. We should. Obviously we are being asked for help because the person cannot qualify for a loan on his or her own.

"It is poor judgment to cosign a friend's note, to become responsible for a neighbor's debt," says the Bible (Proverbs 17:18). How true that is. If the person for whom you cosigned a loan becomes delinquent in or stops making payments, you are the one the creditor will come after for repayment of the loan. Also be aware that your credit report will reflect the loan that you cosigned and could show you over-extended in your debts should you apply for future credit.

When you cosign for a loan, you are required to complete a loan application and qualify for the loan as if you were the primary borrower. Ask yourself, "If the loan is approved and my coborrower defaults can I pay the loan back?"

Sadly, many times I have seen credit reports ruined because individuals cosigned for loans and the original borrower defaults. Most of the time the person who has cosigned for the loan is not notified of any problems until the situation is out of control and her or his credit is ruined.

The best way to avoid a problem if you cosign for a loan is to have the monthly statements sent directly to you. By reviewing the statements monthly, you can see if payments are being made. You also can collect the payment from your cosigner and mail it yourself. That way you know the payment is being made.

DAN'S STORY

Dan and his wife want to refinance their home. When they completed their loan application a credit report was run. Dan's credit report had several late payments on an automobile account. At first he couldn't remember what account that was, then realized that it was a loan he had cosigned for his son.

His son had run into some financial problems and made the payments late on several occasions. He hoped his father wouldn't find out, but the secret came out on the credit report.

I instructed Dan to write a letter to the lender he was trying to get the new loan from, explaining the situation. The lender requested copies of 12 months of his son's cancelled checks for the car payments. With the letter and copies of the cancelled checks, Dan was able to refinance his home.

Dan contacted the loan company who financed the car and instructed the company to send all the monthly statements to his address. By doing this, he was able to monitor that the payments were being made on time and protect his credit.

INSURANCE LIABILITY

Q. *My husband and I cosigned for an automobile loan for our daughter. If she gets in an accident, can the other party come after us for damages?*

The first thing to do is check with your insurance agent. If your daughter was involved in an automobile accident, there is a strong probability that you could be involved in a lawsuit if your daughter's insurance policy didn't cover the costs of the accident. If the other party discovered your name on the registration or loan documents, your name may be added to the lawsuit to improve their chances of recovering their losses.

If your daughter still lives at home or is at college and her insurance is under your automobile policy, you and your husband definitely would be liable. If your daughter lives in a separate household and has her own insurance policy in her name, you probably would not be liable for any damages.

REPOSSESSED CAR

Q. *I cosigned on a car loan for my son. He didn't make the payments and the car was repossessed. My credit has been ruined. What can I do to improve my credit report?*

Anytime you cosign for a loan you are taking a huge risk. The best thing that you could do is get a copy of your credit reports from the three major credit reporting agencies. If the repossession is listed on the credit reports, send a letter to the creditor who repossessed the car and tell it your side of the story.

The creditor may want to make an agreement for you to repay any losses that it had when it sold the car. Ask the creditor to remove your name from the loan and any future liability, as well as remove the repossession from your credit report. If the creditor agrees, get the agreement in writing before making any payments.

Wait four weeks and request another copy of your credit reports. If the loan company has not removed or corrected the entry, send each of the credit reporting agencies a copy of the agreement and proof of your payment. If this does not resolve your reporting problem, you can add a 100-word statement to your credit report describing your side of the story.

CHAPTER 12

COMMUNICATING AND NEGOTIATING WITH CREDITORS

When financial problems occur, your first instinct is to bury your head in the sand and hope the bills will go away. The unfortunate thing is that even if your income has suddenly dropped or ceased, the bills keep arriving.

The worst thing you can do is not communicate with each creditor about your situation. It is better for you to contact your creditor first by telephone or letter before the creditor calls you. The longer you wait to contact the creditor, the more serious the situation will become. Always make the first call.

Prior to calling the creditor, review your finances and evaluate what payments you can pay. Put your proposed payments on paper so you can review your finances with the creditor. Don't pay something you can't afford. Once you have made a commitment to pay, it is important that you stick to the terms of the agreement. If you don't, the creditor will find it difficult to trust you in the future. Any agreement that you make with the creditor, put it in writing and send it certified mail with a return receipt. Request that the creditor send you a confirmation of your agreement.

Many times when a creditor feels that it may not be paid in full, it will settle for a dollar amount less than the balance. Usually the creditor's settlement offer is more than you can afford. When going through a financial crisis, you must make a realistic determination of how long you think you will be going through it. Be sure you keep enough cash for your basic essential living expenses.

Once your financial crisis is over, negotiate with each creditor to settle the unpaid account. If you are not comfortable doing this, ask a friend or relative to negotiate on your behalf. Your credit report is already ruined. You have nothing to lose by trying to settle your accounts for less than the balance. As part of the negotiation, ask the creditor to remove any negative entries or correct the entries to read "paid in full."

SAM'S STORY

Sam contacted my office in a panic. He had just been served papers for a lawsuit from a credit card company that he owed money to. Sam owned his own business and was incorporated, though he was not an officer. Sam showed no assets of his own. The business was not doing well and he had several unexpected emergencies that drained his cash flow. All of his credit cards fell behind.

When Sam and I went over his situation, he didn't realize how much he owed until we reviewed his credit report.

As Sam and I reviewed his credit report and sorted through his file of collection letters, we discovered two other pending lawsuits that needed to be addressed immediately.

Because time was of the essence in responding to these three lawsuits, Sam and I devised a plan. Sam had $5,000 in accounts receivable that he knew he would have within 60 days. With the three lawsuits pending, I contacted all three attorneys and offered a settlement for each creditor. One of the lawsuits was for $5,000 and was settled for $2,300. The second lawsuit was for $3,000 and was settled for $1,200. The third lawsuit was for $3,500 and was settled for $1,500. Sam saved a total of $6,000 with these settlements and the lawsuits were withdrawn.

The remaining creditors that Sam owed were also offered less money. Some of the creditors took his offer, while other creditors did not.

It is going to take Sam a long time to get back on his feet, however by negotiating with his creditors he was able to avoid a bankruptcy.

A SETTLED ACCOUNT ON MY CREDIT REPORT

Q.　*I paid off a bank loan for less than the amount owed. The bank agreed to this and listed my account as settled on my credit report. What does this mean? Would another credit grantor view this as a negative entry?*

Any time you pay off a debt for less than the amount due, the creditor will report to the credit bureau that the account was "settled." This entry could be viewed as a negative entry by a potential creditor who would see that you did not pay your obligation according to the original terms of your contract.

When you are negotiating with a creditor and offering to settle your account for less money, make it part of the settlement that the creditor reports the account as "paid in full" to all the credit bureaus. If they agree to do this, get it in writing before you make any payment. Trying to go back after you have paid the account and get the creditor to change the "settled" entry could be difficult.

THE CREDITORS WON'T LISTEN

Q. *I'm on a very tight budget and the bill collectors keep calling. I explain my situation to them, but it doesn't seem to make any difference. What can I do?*

One thing you need to remember when you are faced with past due bills and cannot make the payments required, is to have a plan. The first thing you must do is write down a list of your essential bills. For example, house or rent payment, food, electricity, water, transportation etc. These bills must always be paid first. Too often, when a person falls into trouble, the most persistent creditor will intimidate you into paying its bill rather than paying your essential living bills. Remember, your credit report is already damaged, so don't hurt your family by not keeping enough cash to pay your essential bills. Your credit rating is not going to be improved. The best thing to do after your essential bills are paid is to then analyze what you have left and distribute what you can to the creditors.

The second option would be to try to negotiate a payment plan with your creditors that you can live with. After you know how much you need to pay all your essential bills, add up your nonessential bills—credit cards, charge cards, medical bills, etc. Can you pay 2 percent of each bill per month to each creditor? If you can, write down each creditor's name with the proposed monthly payment. Make this offer to each creditor. Some may accept it, and some may not; however, send the proposed payment to each of the creditors each month anyway. Most creditors will deposit your checks. Once you can increase the payments, do it, but only after your essential bills are paid.

If you are unable to pay anything towards your nonessential creditors now, pay something when you can.

SETTLING FOR LESS

Q. *I'm on Medicaid with medical bills. The credit card companies are indicating they are willing to take less money for payments. Why are they willing to do that?*

Your medical bills must be quite large for the creditors to be so eager to take less of a payment. Their fear is that you will file for bankruptcy. Any outstanding bill that is owed when filing for a bankruptcy must be named. Most of the time the creditor will not receive anything if the item is discharged through a bankruptcy.

By being willing to take smaller payments the creditors are happy to receive something from you instead of nothing at all.

Keep the arrangements you have made with the creditors. When your income has increased, apply more money towards your monthly payments to bring the balance down.

I CAN'T MAKE MY CAR PAYMENT

Q. *I can't make my car payment this month. Several things happened this month and I am running short of funds. Will the bank repossess my car if I miss a payment?*

A bank can repossess your car if you are one day late making your payment, however, this doesn't happen very often. The bank really doesn't want your car.

First, contact the lender who financed your car. Explain your situation. Some lenders will allow you to defer one payment per year. That means that the lender will allow you to miss one payment and add the missed payment to the end of your contract. For example if you had a 48-month contract, it would be extended to 49 months.

Other lenders may allow you to make interest-only payments for a specific period of time. The principal is added to the end of your contract and is due with your final payment.

Occasionally the lender will consider allowing you to refinance your car. The contract would be longer so you would be paying more in interest; however, the monthly payments would be lower.

If none of these options are workable, sell the car. Take the money and pay off the loan. Use whatever you have left to purchase an inexpensive car. This would be better than a repossession.

A repossession on your credit report would make it more difficult to qualify in the future for another car. Always try to preserve your credit rating.

PAY OR BE CHARGED OFF

Q. *Six months ago I was laid off my job. I have not been able to make my credit card payments. I have explained my situation to the creditors but they keep calling me daily. Several companies indicated that they would accept a discount on my balance if I pay them by the end of the month. If I don't agree my accounts will be charged off. Why are the creditors now willing to work with me?*

After trying to collect on an account for six months, most creditors will automatically charge off the account. A charge-off is a bad mark on your credit report. Even after charging off an account, most creditors will turn the account over to a collection agency.

As your account becomes close to the six-month period when it will be charged off (but rarely before), many creditors are willing to settle the account for less. They figure collecting something is better than nothing.

It always amazes me how unrealistic a creditor's offer to settle is. If you can't make a small minimum payment, how could you pay a large lump sum? Should you come into any extra cash, it is better for you to make the offer based on what you could pay, *after* paying essential living expenses.

If the creditor doesn't accept, move on to another creditor with the same offer who will accept it.

SETTLING WITH THE IRS

Q. *I owe the IRS $20,000 in back taxes. These taxes are from three years ago. The balance keeps going up because of interest and penalties. Will the IRS negotiate with me to settle this tax bill?*

The IRS has an Offer In Compromise program to allow taxpayers to pay their tax bills off at a reduction. The IRS has its own criteria on what it will accept.

You hear stories of the IRS accepting ten cents on the dollar; however, unless an offer is made you will never know what it will accept. The IRS will look at your earning ability, what your income currently is, how likely it is that you can ever pay the tax bill off, and your current financial statements.

If you contact the IRS directly, it will mail you the necessary forms to complete for you to make an offer in compromise. Tax attorneys, accountants, and enrolled agents can work on your behalf to make an offer. If the IRS accepts your offer, be prepared to pay it in full. Make sure you understand all the requirements that you are agreeing to for this settlement.

Sean Melvin's book, *Settle Your Tax Debt* (Dearborn, 1998) explains the offer in compromise program in detail.

MEDICAL BILLS

Q. *My doctor is threatening to turn my account over to a collection agency. I have tried making small payments but still owe a bill of $800. I have a small amount of money set aside. Should I offer to pay the bill for a less amount of money?*

If your doctor's office is threatening to turn your bill over to a collection agency, I would immediately make an offer. Explain to the doctor your hardship. Offer to pay the doctor three payments of $100 each to settle the account in full. If the doctor agrees, get a letter stating your agreement before you make any payments.

When a bill goes to collection, depending on the arrangement with the collection company, the doctor may only collect 30 to 50 percent of the balance. The collection agency would keep the difference.

Many times a doctor will waive 20 percent of the bill if the remaining balance is paid by your insurance company. It never hurts to negotiate; it can save both you and your doctor months of frustration.

RE-AGING AN ACCOUNT

Q. *My son became very ill and I was unable to work. Several of my credit cards became delinquent. The creditors are calling me daily. Two companies indicated that they would reduce my interest rate, bring my account current, and remove any delinquencies if I would mail them three post-dated checks spaced 30 days apart. What does this mean?*

Many times creditors will offer to re-age an account by accepting three post-dated checks in return for a lower interest rate. Bringing your account current could be a blessing in disguise. This agreement benefits you only if you can afford it. By the creditor offering to remove any delinquencies from your account your credit report will be greatly improved. It is important that you get any agreement you make with the creditor in writing to make sure it holds up its end of the bargain.

If you know you can't afford the three payments, don't send anything. It would be a worse situation if your checks bounced.

Many creditors will offer to re-age your account to help you get back on track. Once you take a plunge downhill, it is hard to bring your accounts current. Re-aging an account is the best way to do it if you can afford to.

I MISSED THE PAYMENT ARRANGEMENT

Q. *I fell behind in several of my credit card payments. I had to make special payment arrangements on several of my accounts. Unfortunately, I was able to make only two of the arranged payments and fell behind again. I am afraid to contact the companies to try and make new arrangements. Should I just leave it alone and wait to see what the companies' next move is?*

Never wait to see what a company is going to do. Lack of communication will only expedite any action a company may take. Contact the creditor immediately. Prior to contacting it, make sure you have another payment plan to offer.

Explain that you set the payments too high for the income you have to support them. Make a new offer of payments that you can afford.

Most of the time creditors will work with you. The creditor wants to see monthly activity on your account. As you get closer to paying the account off, try to negotiate for the creditor to remove any derogatory information that is being reported on your credit report. If the company agrees to removing the derogatory remarks from your credit report, get it in writing. Should the company fail to keep its promise, submit the letter to the credit reporting agencies for them to update their records.

DEBT MANAGEMENT SERVICES

Q. *Are there any companies or resources that can help me with my debts and be an intermediary for me with my creditors?*

There are several resources available to individuals who need to manage their credit. Self-help books can help you budget and manage your credit. My book, *The Insider's Guide to Managing Your Credit,* offers strategies for getting out of debt, as well for managing your bills. The Internet is another resource.

Consumer Credit Counseling Service is a nonprofit organization that evaluates your income and expenses and makes suggestions for budgeting and debt repayment. If your situation calls for further service, CCCS also will intervene with your creditors to help reduce your debt, lower your interest rate, and act as a mediator between you and your creditors.

If you want assistance from CCCS, refer to the white pages of your telephone directory, or call its national toll-free number, 800-388-CCCS(2227).

Other debt management groups are Debt Counselors of America (800-680-3328 or www.dca.org), and Bankcard Holders of America (524 Branch Dr., Salem, VA 24153), which, for a small fee, will run a computerized analysis of your debts and recommend the most efficient way to repay them.

CHAPTER 13

COLLECTION AGENCIES

Collection agencies can be ruthless in their methods of collection. Many individuals feel intimidated and fearful of collection agencies.

An agency is retained when the original creditor has given up on you. A collection agency may purchase the debt from the original creditor for a large discount, or it may take a percentage of what is collected and then pay the difference to the original creditor.

To avoid intimidation, know your legal rights concerning collection agencies. The 1977 Fair Debt Collection Practice Act protects consumers from unethical bill collectors. To receive a copy of this law, write to the Federal Trade Commission (which enforces the provisions of the act), Sixth and Pennsylvania Ave. NW, Washington, DC 20580.

Whenever you deal with a collection agency, have a plan and don't allow the agency to intimidate you into making payments you can't afford. It is not uncommon for a collection agency to continuously call you and send you letters demanding that you pay off the debt.

A collection agency knows if it can get you to respond within 60 days, the chances of collecting the amount due is the highest. The more time between the first contact and collecting the account, the less chance the collection agency has of collecting.

As the months go by, the calls and letters become fewer and fewer. The approach changes, too. The first three months the collection agency will come on strong and not be open to any negotiations or settlements. As time passes, the collection company will be offering you a substantial discount to settle the account, figuring that something is better than nothing.

SUSAN'S STORY

Susan was in a panic when she called my office. She was a single mother and had lost her job. It took Susan several months to find another job and she had to take a pay cut. Her bills had fallen behind and several accounts were turned over to a collection agency.

That morning a collection agency called Susan at work. The collector said that if she didn't pay the bill within 24 hours by a cashiers' check that the collection agency would turn her account over to its attorney, who would enforce the collection action. The collection agency could have her wages garnished and she could go to jail.

Susan didn't have the money to pay the collection agency. She pleaded with them to work with her but the collection agency said she had to pay the bill in full.

As I listened to Susan, I could feel her fears and anxiety. It's not the first time I had heard a horror story relating to collection agency tactics.

I told Susan, "Don't let the collection agency intimidate you. If you don't have the money, don't pay it. Collection agencies are notorious for using fear tactics." As I felt Susan's tension lessen, I told her, "Collection agencies can't garnish your wages unless there is a judgment against you. You would have to be served papers for a lawsuit. At that time you could try to settle the account. Most of the time a collection agency never sues; they only threaten. Tell the collection agency your employer doesn't allow you to receive personal calls at your work. Once you have told the collection agency this, they can't call you at your employment."

As I spoke with Susan, she started to feel stronger in dealing with the collection agency. Knowledge empowers you to handle situations in unfamiliar territory.

Collection agencies have a way of playing mind games with people. During a weak moment when you let your guard down, panic will seize you.

Susan called me again the next morning, still a little uncertain of her position. She said, "Just tell me one thing. Can I go to jail?" I quickly said, "No, there is no debtors' prison." That was all she needed to hear, and we quickly hung up. The pressure was off her and her fears removed so she could handle her problems with her new knowledge.

THREATENING JUDGMENT

Q. *Can a collection agency get a judgment against me?*

A collection agency cannot represent or imply that the nonpayment of any debt will result in an arrest, garnishment, or attachment, providing the collection agency does not intend to take legal action. The threat to take any action that cannot legally be taken or that is not intended to be taken is a violation of the consumer's rights.

If the collection agency has purchased the debt from the original creditor, it can enforce a lawsuit against you to collect the debt. If it does go to court and you lose the case, a judgment can be made against you and it can try to collect the debt. It must follow the court's procedures when trying to collect.

If the collection agency has not purchased the debt from the original creditor and is only receiving a percentage of the amount collected, it must follow the instructions from the original creditor. The collection agency cannot sue you. Only the original creditor can initiate a lawsuit.

FINANCE CHARGES

Q. *How much interest can a collection agency legally charge?*

A collection agency cannot add on any finance charge or service fee in collecting a debt unless the extra charge is authorized in the agreement creating the debt, which the consumer signed.

When you complete a credit application, or information sheet for a doctor, dentist, hospital, or any type of credit, there is a disclaimer usually at the bottom of the information sheet. It is usually in small print and will have a statement that by signing the contract or application, you are agreeing to pay what is owed, or you will pay for services rendered. If you do not pay what is owed, the credit grantor has a right to add a finance charge (the percentage or amount must be stated) to the outstanding bill. By signing this, you are agreeing to pay the finance charge. If the account is turned over to a collection agency, you already have agreed to pay the finance charge.

If you never signed an agreement indicating you would pay a finance charge, you do not have to pay one.

Always keep copies of what you sign. Without your copies to refer back to, you would never know if the company was adding on charges that you are not obligated to pay.

If a collection agency states that you owe a finance charge or interest on a debt, tell it to send you the original document you signed.

CALLS AT WORK

Q.   *The collection agency keeps calling me at work. They even told my employer that I owe them money. My employer is upset about these calls. How can I stop the collection agency from calling me at work?*

A collection agency is not allowed to discuss with anyone other than you the purpose for their call. If they do it is a violation of the Fair Collection Practice Act.

A collection agency will try to call you at work. The collection agency has gotten your work telephone number from your original application.

The Fair Debt Collection Practice Act gives you the right to tell the collection agency to stop all telephone calls to your work. You must tell the collection agency that your employer does not permit personal calls. Once you have told them this, the collection agency may not contact you at your place of business. If the collection agency continues to call you at work and discusses your situation with anyone other than yourself you should file a complaint with the Federal Trade Commission.

DAUGHTER IS A MINOR

Q. *We are trying to refinance our home. A collection account appeared on my credit report for my daughter. It was a medical bill. My daughter is a minor.*

The reason your daughter's account appeared on your credit report is because she is a minor and you evidently signed a form at the doctor's office that you are the one responsible for paying her medical bill.

A child under the age of 18 years is considered a minor. A doctor will require a parent or guardian's signature for the one responsible for the payment of services rendered.

If the doctor's bill is not paid and the doctor turns the account over to an outside collection agency, the parent or legal guardian who signed the form authorizing the services will be the one who is reported on the credit report by the collection agency.

DISPUTED ACCOUNT

Q. *I received a letter from a collection agency indicating I owe money on an old account. I do not believe I owe this. What can I do?*

Federal law gives you the right to verify any debt you feel is not valid. Whenever a collection agency sends you a statement that you owe money, the statement must provide "the amount of the debt, the name of the creditor to whom the bill is owed, and a statement showing that unless the consumer within 30 days after receipt of the notice, disputes the validity of the debt, or any portion of the debt, it will be assumed to be valid by the debt collector."

If you do not write a letter disputing the debt the collection agency will continue to pursue collection. Write your letter disputing this debt within the 30 days that you received it. Send it certified mail with a return receipt requested.

The collection agency must send you verification of the debt, and any documentation related to the debt. It is not allowed to communicate with you prior to verification of the debt that you are disputing.

ONE ACCOUNT, SEVERAL COLLECTION AGENCIES

Q. *I had an account that was charged off. The original creditor
    turned the account over to a collection agency. I never paid the
    collection agency and now there is a new collection agency
    involved. What is going on?*

Many times after an original creditor has charged off an account, it will
turn the account over to an outside collection agency. The agreement may
specify the length of time the collection agency has to collect the debt. If
the agency doesn't collect, the creditor may replace one agency with another.

Usually when a new collection agency is noted in the credit report, the
old collection agency is deleted.

If you wish to settle the account, you must contact the new collection
agency.

THE DEBT WAS SOLD

Q. *Several years ago I had two accounts that were charged off. They
    both were turned over to a collection agency. I never paid the
    collection agency and was just notified from a third company that
    it bought the debt and would work with me to help me reestablish
    my credit. Who are these people?*

There are several companies purchasing debts from the original creditors for pennies on the dollar. Usually these accounts are several years old
and the original creditor will take what it can get and sell the debt at a discount. The original creditor will notate a zero balance on your credit report and that the debt was sold. The entry is still noted as negative.

The new company that purchased the debt will put a negative entry on
your credit report. On the credit report the entry will also list the original
creditor and the date of the last activity on the account.

When the new company makes initial contact with you regarding the
debt, the conversation will go something like this, "Hello, I am Mr. B from
XYZ Company. We have recently purchased your debt from ABC Company and want to help you reestablish your credit. We are willing to give

you new credit if you pay 50 percent of the debt now and start making regular payments. By doing this you will get rid of the negative entry and be able to start rebuilding your credit. How does that sound? When can we expect your payment?" Every company has its own approach to trying to collect; however, the damage is already done on your credit report from the original creditor. The new company can discount as much as it wants because it paid such a small amount for the debt. You would have to determine by reviewing your financial situation if you could begin making payments to this new company. The new company could have the original creditor delete the negative entry on your credit report.

MEDICAL BILLS MY INSURANCE COMPANY SHOULD PAY

Q. *I was applying for a credit card and was denied the credit. When I received a copy of my credit report I discovered two collection accounts on my credit report for medical bills that my insurance company was supposed to pay. What can I do? The collection agency only wants its money and won't cooperate.*

This seems to be a common problem. Some hospitals and doctors' offices will charge off an account if it has not been paid within a certain time. This is even if a payment from the insurance company is pending.

Most of the time the accounts are sent to an outside collection agency that reports the account on your credit report.

Contact the doctor or hospital before contacting the collection agency to try and settle the account. You might even try sending a check to see if it is cashed. If the check clears, contact the collection agency and let it know the account has been paid.

If the doctor or hospital agrees to accept payment directly from you rather than the collection agency, it should contact the collection agency once they receive the payment to remove the account from your credit report.

If the doctor or hospital do not cooperate with you, try to get the insurance company involved to back up your explanation.

The collection agency will only take instructions from the original creditor who is the doctor or hospital. If the collection agency gives you a hard time and begins harassing you, file a complaint with the Federal Trade Commission. Send a copy of the letter to the collection agency to let them know you mean business.

STOP HARRASSMENT

Q. *I have been getting telephone calls from a collection agency early mornings and late at night. When they call, I feel like they are harassing me. They have even threatened me with being arrested. What can I do? Can they do this?*

No! A collection agency is regulated by the Fair Debt Collection Practice Act. This law was designed to protect you from unfair practices by collection agencies. You can request a copy of this law from the Federal Trade Commission.

A collection agency cannot call you before 8:00 AM or after 9:00 PM. If they do they are breaking the law. A collection agency is not allowed to threaten you. You can't be arrested for not paying a bill.

Write a letter to the collection agency telling them that you do not want any further contact. Mail it certified mail with a return receipt. The collection agency is allowed to make one more attempt to collect the bill after receipt of your letter; however, they must notify you of what their intent is to try and collect. From that point on, the collection agency is not allowed to contact you. If they do, make sure you get the name and telephone number of the individual you talk to. File a complaint with the owner of the company, the original creditor, and the Federal Trade Commission.

With any luck the original creditor may drop all collection activity after seeing how the collection agency has broken the law.

CHAPTER 14

BANKRUPTCY

Bankruptcies are at a record high. More and more individuals are being forced into bankruptcy while trying to recover from poor economic conditions: businesses closings, job lay-offs, illnesses, hospitalizations, divorces, etc.

Credit card debt in the United States is at an all-time high. With the problems now facing many individuals, bankruptcy seems to be their only answer. Pressure from creditors is unbearable.

The bill collectors' constant calls and letters demanding money that you don't have is causing you stress, anxiety, marital problems, and sleepless nights. You are afraid to answer your telephone when it rings, wondering if it is another bill collector.

Bankruptcy was not a word in your vocabulary, but now it seems to be your only answer. You need to learn what your options are.

There are three different types of bankruptcy. A Chapter 7 liquidation and a Chapter 13 reorganization are personal bankruptcies. A Chapter 11 bankruptcy is a business reorganization, similar to a Chapter 13. A person must file a Chapter 11 reorganization if his or her debt is higher than the maximum debt for a Chapter 13.

Chapter 7 and Chapter 13 are the types of bankruptcies usually filed by individuals. A Chapter 7—known as a straight bankruptcy—usually will wipe out most of your debts. A Chapter 13 allows you to structure a plan to repay your creditors through the court.

Consult a reputable accountant or bankruptcy attorney about what options you have available to you.

John Ventura's book, *The Bankruptcy Kit* (Dearborn, 1996) is a good resource to learn what your legal rights are in filing a bankruptcy and what you can expect during the process.

JIM AND MARION'S STORY

Jim called my office twice, stressing it was urgent that I call him back. He had to decide that week whether or not to file for bankruptcy.

Jim and his wife Marion pastored a small church. Jim's income was $500 per week. Marion had had a good job, but was recently laid off. They lived rent-free in the parsonage, but they had $30,000 in credit card and installment debt. Their car had been repossessed, so they borrowed money to have the loan reinstated to get the car back. Arguments and strife over finances was leading to a possible break-up of their marriage. It had been more than six months since any credit card payments had been made.

The only payments that were being made were for a car loan, car insurance, and medical insurance. Jim's income alone left a $200 per month shortfall on their expenses.

After discussing their situation, I knew that because of Jim's position with his church, a bankruptcy could be the wrong choice for them.

I explained to them that there was a possibility that their car would have to be returned to the loan company if they proceeded with the bankruptcy. I suggested that they eliminate the car payment by selling the car and use whatever cash they got to pay cash for another car. The insurance premiums could be reduced by raising the deductibles.

Most of the credit card companies had charged off their accounts or they were placed with collection agencies. Even those letters and telephone calls were slowly fading away.

I asked Jim and Marion why they were considering filing for a bankruptcy now. Marion said, "I can't handle the continuous letters and telephone calls. We have changed our telephone number twice and now have our mail sent to another address. I feel like I'm hiding out."

Other than discharging the credit card debts, I saw no benefit to the bankruptcy because their financial situation would remain the same. Because of Jim's job, it would be better to negotiate a future settlement with the creditors when they had more money.

I suggested that Marion and Jim both get part-time jobs to supplement their income during the interim. It was a test of endurance to withstand the telephone calls and letters from the creditors. The telephone calls and letters would slowly come to a halt which would bring relief. Jim and Marion had no assets that the creditors could collect on so the chances of lawsuits were small.

Bankruptcy is not for everyone. Filing for a bankruptcy could definitely damage certain careers. Weigh all the options before filing for a bankruptcy because it is a public record. Negotiating with creditors becomes easier the longer the debt has gone unpaid.

DON'T BELIEVE EVERYTHING YOU HEAR

Q. *I heard if I file a bankruptcy that I can easily get new credit. Is this true?*

Not exactly. I have heard this too; however, all my clients who have filed bankruptcy have had a difficult time reestablishing themselves.

When you are getting ready to meet with the trustee at the bankruptcy court for your final discharge, occasionally some of your creditors will show up to offer you special deals if you pay them off. Many of them will offer to reinstate your line of credit if you pay them off rather than have the account discharged where they will receive nothing. Most people cannot take them up on their offer and the account is then discharged.

KEN AND MARCIE'S STORY

I had been on Michael Reagan's radio talk show discussing issues on credit. Ken called me the next day at my office. He explained that he was $60,000 in debt and wanted my opinion if he should file for a bankruptcy or get a second trust deed on his home. Ken was a salesperson and had just changed jobs. He had a good income and some equity in his home. I told Ken that I felt we should try to get a second loan on his home to pay the debt off, but first he would have to complete a loan application.

Once I received his loan application, I had a credit report run. Ken and Marcie's credit was perfect. Every creditor reported an excellent credit rating; however, something didn't look right. I totaled the balances and I discovered that Ken and Marcie's debts came to $160,000. This didn't include their mortgage. I was stunned. I couldn't understand how Ken and Marcie didn't know that they owed that much.

Unfortunately, I was the one who had to make the telephone call to inform Ken and Marcie that they were $160,000 in debt. As the telephone rang I took a deep breath and said, "Ken, you are not $60,000 in debt, but you owe $160,000 between your credit card bills and vehicles." There was a long silence on the other end of the telephone. Softly, Ken said, "I guess things can get away from you without you ever realizing it." His next question was, "What should we do?"

Ken and Marcie were a catastrophe ready to happen. All the warning signs were there of a financial crash.

I reviewed his loan application, got a value on his property, and played with the figures to try and get a second trust deed—even a 125 percent loan against the house—but his debt ratios were still too high to qualify.

With such a high debt and not being able to get Ken and Marcie a loan, I suggested they consult a bankruptcy attorney. There didn't appear to be any way out for them.

WHAT CREDIT TO SAVE

Q. *It looks as though my husband and I will need to file for bankruptcy. Is there any way to save our credit rating?*

The best suggestion I could give you would be to keep one or two of your credit cards current at all times. Before you file for your bankruptcy, try to pay the cards off. Put them in a safe deposit box or drawer so you won't use them. If you have two credit cards through the same company, either pay them off or have them both discharged. If you pay one card off and have the other credit card discharged through the bankruptcy, the chances are that the credit card company will cancel the other card. Try to keep the cards with the lowest fees and interest rates.

When you make the list of all your outstanding creditors, you would not have to list the cards that are paid off. After your bankruptcy has been discharged by the court, you now have one or two accounts that are in good standing. When you are trying to reestablish yourself in the credit world, this will look good on your credit report. Any future credit will depend on your payment history since your bankruptcy.

SINGLE MOTHER

Q. *I am a single mother with two children and a $15,000 credit card debt. I have fallen behind in my payments and am one month behind in my mortgage payment. Should I file for a bankruptcy?*

Before rushing into filing for a bankruptcy, you need to analyze your total situation.

Get a copy of your credit report from all three of the major credit reporting agencies—Experian, Trans Union, and Equifax. Analyze each of the entries and see what the creditors are reporting. Have they charged off the accounts as bad debts, or have they placed the accounts into a collection status? What you're trying to determine is what damage has the creditors done on your credit report. If the damage is severe, a bankruptcy will only add one more derogatory statement which will haunt you for the next ten years.

If your credit report is damaged, then ride the storm. Set priorities as to what you are going to pay. No matter how loud the creditors are yelling, your first priority is to survive. Your house payment should always be paid first. Then your utilities, food, and automobile. These are essential to your survival. Whatever you have left can go to the creditors. Remember your credit report is already ruined.

A bankruptcy should only be considered if you stand to lose your home (which would only slow the process), or your debt is more than $20,000 and there is no possible way to pay the debt back in the future.

Your debt may seem high, but to take a drastic step and file for bankruptcy will only quiet the creditors. The end result will cause a worse credit rating. Eventually the creditors will quit harassing you. It is a test of endurance on your part. Hang in there and try to bring your house payment current.

TAX LIENS DISCHARGED

Q. *Five years ago our business went bad. We have tax liens that amount to more than $100,000, two judgments totaling $140,000, and $60,000 in credit card debt. Can we file for a bankruptcy and get the tax liens discharged?*

Tax liens usually are not dischargeable in a bankruptcy. If the tax liens are more than four-and-one-half-years-old, they may be dischargeable under certain circumstances.

Whenever anyone has a problem with back taxes and are contemplating a bankruptcy, it is best to see an attorney or accountant who specializes in tax law to advise you.

Under most circumstances, judgments and unsecured credit card debt are dischargeable through a bankruptcy. With debts that are so high, unless your income increases high enough to pay these debts off, a bankruptcy would be your only sense of relief and a new start.

IF I CHANGE MY MIND

Q. *Can I change my mind after I file for a Chapter 7 personal bankruptcy? What will happen?*

Yes, you can change your mind and have the case dismissed; however, once the bankruptcy is filed it becomes a public notice which is picked up by the credit reporting agencies and becomes a part of your credit history. You would want to make sure that the credit report shows the bankruptcy dismissed. The bankruptcy filing and dismissal would show up on your credit report every time a credit report is run. The entry would remain on your credit report for up to ten years from the date it was filed. You could add a letter of explanation on your credit report explaining the situation.

Another thing you could do would be to explain your situation to a new prospective credit grantor prior to completing an application. If it views the entry as negative and will decline your credit application, don't authorize a credit report to be run on you. The rejected inquiry will hurt your chances with another creditor.

CHAPTER 13 OR 7?

Q. *I have credit card debt of more than $60,000. I was on disability and my income dropped. I am back on the job and my income is picking up; however, I have fallen three months behind in making my payments. I want to be able to pay these bills off, but I'm having a hard time catching up. Is there a way to reduce my payments?*

Being $60,000 in credit card debt will take you over 20 years to pay back by making minimum payments. The fact that you are already behind in making your payments will make it more difficult to bring the accounts current.

A Chapter 13 bankruptcy is known as a wage earner program. It allows you to set the payments that you can afford. It must be approved by the trustee of the court. Once the payments are set, you would continue to make the payments to the trustee for three to five years, depending on the program the trustee approves.

At the end of the three to five year period when your final payment is made, any remaining balances that you have will be discharged. No further payments will be required and the debts will be considered paid in full.

If you elect to file for a Chapter 7 bankruptcy, the unsecured debts, if approved by the trustee may be discharged. Any items that secured debts would have to be surrendered or special arrangements made by the court for repayment.

REAFFIRMATION

Q. *I am considering filing for a bankruptcy. Can I keep any of my credit cards and not have to give them up?*

If you owe balances on any credit cards or any outstanding balances on any debt that you owe, you must declare it in your bankruptcy petition. If you have a zero balance on any credit cards or lines of credit, you do not have to declare it.

If you file for a bankruptcy, some of the creditors may ask you to reaffirm your debt with them. A *reaffirmation* means that the creditor will close the old account and open a new account transferring your balance to the new account. You would then make payments on the account.

By doing a reaffirmation on a credit card, the creditor will usually allow you to use the line of credit that you established. Prior to doing a reaffirmation, get the creditor to give you a statement in writing listing the terms, interest, fees, and credit limit. Never be late in making your payments on any accounts you have reaffirmed. If you fall delinquent in any of your payments after your bankruptcy and it is reported on your credit report it will hurt your chances of reestablishing new credit.

YOUR FINANCIAL FUTURE

CHAPTER **15**

GETTING OUT OF DEBT

Most of us have the dream of being debt free. To realize that dream, you must have a plan and sacrifice the things you want today. In other words, most people aren't willing to sacrifice little luxuries such as eating out, fast food stops, trips to the ATM machines and losing track of where the money goes, entertainment, memberships to the gyms, expensive coffee breaks and so on in exchange for no debt.

By giving up some of the little luxuries you spend your money on, the money saved can be used to pay off your debts. If you counted every penny you spent for 30 days on every purchase you made and every bill that was paid, you would be surprised at where your money went. It will then be easy to cut back and use the money that you waste to pay your bills off. It may take several months or years to become debt free. Knowing you have a goal and a target date will help you meet your goal.

One man heard me on two separate occasions talking about getting out of debt. He purchased my book, *The Insiders Guide to Managing Your Credit,* and followed the guidelines to get out of debt. One year later he called in when I was on another radio show. He said that one year ago he was $15,000 in debt. But after purchasing my book and putting a plan together, he had reduced his debt to $2,500. It was rewarding for me to hear his testimony, but also a reinforcement showing how a plan could help almost anyone to become debt free.

GLEN'S STORY

Glen was self-employed and owed $45,000 in credit card debt. He owned his home and was paying an 11 percent interest rate on his mortgage.

Glen was self-employed and his income was inconsistent. When he called my office, he was distraught. He didn't know how much longer he could hold on and make the payments on his credit cards and home. He thought by selling his home he could get enough money to pay off his debts and move into a cheaper home. Selling his home wasn't what he really wanted to do because he had a young family and had lived in his home for more than ten years.

I had Glen list all of his monthly payments, including his credit card bills and house payment. They totaled $4,600 per month. Glen also indicated that he had fallen behind in some of his payments including his house payment during the past year. Everything was presently current; however, he didn't know how long he could hold on.

I got an appraisal of what Glen's house was worth and the amount of debt he had. I figured out that Glen could save $900 per month by refinancing his house at a lower rate and taking cash out to pay off all the credit card debts. (Because Glen had some problems on his credit report, his interest rate was slightly higher than a regular refinancing, but still lower than what he had been paying.)

Because Glen no longer had any credit card debt, I suggested that he add extra money to his house payment (marked "pay to principal") so he could pay his house off in less than 30 years.

Glen was relieved that he didn't have to sell his house and was able to save such a large amount per month. It took the pressure off him so he could build his business up.

SYMPTOMS OF TOO MUCH DEBT

Q. *Is there a way to tell if you have too much debt. We are newly-weds and don't want to fall into that trap. Any suggestions?*

The best way to stay out of debt is to pay your credit cards bills off in full at the end of each month. People lose control by not keeping track of what they are charging.

Most people can afford to pay 10 percent of their net income to installment debt, not including their mortgage payments. If you pay out more than 15 percent to installment debt, you need to cut back. More than 20 percent being paid out to installment debt could result in financial problems. It is important to have a budget sheet that you fill out every month to make sure you are not paying out more than 10 percent of your income towards installment debt. If you are, make adjustments for the following month to reduce your debt.

It is important that both of you know exactly what is going on with your finances so there are no surprises. Review your budget sheet together once a month and try to live within your income.

MOVE YOUR HIGH-INTEREST CREDIT CARD BALANCES

Q. *I have several credit cards that I am paying on. The interest rates range from 14 percent to 19 percent. I don't feel like I'll ever get these cards paid off. Are there any suggestions you could give me to get these debts paid off sooner?*

The first thing you need to do is to make a list of all your credit cards. Include in your list the payment, balance, interest rate, and unused credit limit.

Once you have your list, analyze if you have room to move your balances from your high interest rate cards to your lower interest rate cards. If you do, take a cash advance and move the high interest rate balance to the lower interest rate card. For example if the credit card you have with 14 percent interest rate has a balance of $1,000 and a credit limit of $5,000, and you owe $3,000 on the credit card with a 19 percent interest rate, get a cash advance from your credit card with the 14 percent interest rate for $3,000. Pay off the $3,000 balance on the 19 percent interest rate credit card. You now would owe $4,000 on the 14 percent interest rate credit card. With the payment you were making on the 19 percent interest rate card, add that to the payment you are making on the 14 percent interest rate credit card. Continue adding the additional payment until the balance is paid off. You are saving 5 percent interest on 75 percent of your debt. Your balance will come down rapidly because the extra payments will apply towards the principal balance. You also will reduce the amount of years you'll be paying on the credit card.

UP TO MY CREDIT LIMITS

Q. *I am up to my credit limits on all my credit cards. It feels as if I will never be able to pay these cards off. My total debt is $12,000. Any suggestions on paying these off? I don't own a home.*

By maxing out your credit limits and only making minimum payments it could take you many years to pay the balances off.

For example, if you have a credit card balance of $2,000 and make only a minimum payment per month, it would take you more than 16½ years to pay the credit card off. This is assuming you never make another purchase with the credit card. The interest you would pay at the end of the 16½ years would be $2,504.62 which would be in addition to the $2,000 which would total $4,504.62. That is a lot of money to pay for purchases that are now outdated.

Based on the original $2,000 balance, if you pay $5 per month over your minimum payment, you will save $738.59 and eliminate more than five years from the loan. If you pay $10 per month over your minimum payment, you will save $1,113.70 and eliminate more than eight years from the loan. By simply paying over and above your monthly payment, the principal balance will be reduced and you will pay the debt off quicker.

Be sure to not charge again on the credit cards that you are paying down. You will only be starting the cycle over again.

When your balances are low enough, begin transferring the higher interest rate credit card balances to the lower interest rate credit cards and continue to add your extra payments.

LOW INTEREST RATE TEASERS

Q. *My goal this year is to try and get out of debt as soon as possible. I have four credit cards that are charged to their limits. I have been receiving these low interest rate credit card applications*

*offering rates of 4.9 percent. Would I be wise to apply for these
cards so I can pay my credit cards off quicker?*

Credit card companies are saturating the mailboxes with these teaser
rate credit card offers. Usually the interest rates offered with these credit
cards are only good for six months to one year. These cards are usually
available to you as long as you move a balance over from another card.

By moving your credit cards to the lower interest rate card I would suggest you continue to make the same payments you were on the higher interest rate card. Cancel the credit card that you moved over to the low
interest rate card.

Keep in mind that you will need to know all the terms of the teaser rate
card and be on alert to the expiration of the low interest. As you come
upon the expiration date, contact the bank and ask them to extend the low
interest rate for another six months. If they don't agree to this, look for another lower rate card to transfer the balance. Follow the same procedure
as you did with the first card by canceling the credit card that you moved.
By continuing to make the extra payments, your balance will be zero in
no time and you will have saved money.

MORTGAGE REDUCTION PLAN

Q. *I want to pay my house off early. We have a 30-year-fixed-interest-
rate loan. How much extra should I pay to reduce the years of my
loan?*

One extra house payment per year can cut a 30 year loan into a 15 to
17 year loan. You can divide one house payment by 12 months and add
that to your regular payment.

Most of the mortgage payment is paid towards interest, however when
you pay over and above the monthly payment, specify that it be applied to
the principal.

By making extra payments each month you will save possibly hundreds
of thousands of dollars during the life of your loan and have your house
paid off early.

TOO MUCH DEBT—NOT ENOUGH CASH

Q. *Our debt is higher than our income. We own a home and are*
    having problems making ends meet. We do have some equity in
    our home, but I don't think refinancing will solve our problems.
    Any suggestions?

If refinancing your home is not an option, perhaps you need to consider
selling your home and paying off all your debts. Use the money you have
left over to purchase a smaller home with less of a house payment.

Sometimes it's hard to make a drastic decision like selling your home;
however, the longer you allow yourself to get deeper into debt, the harder
it will be to solve your problem. It is better to act quickly rather than wait
until you fall behind in making your payments and your credit rating is affected. This way you can get into another property being debt free with
only one house payment to make.

If you need to raise cash in a hurry to offset some bills, take an inven-
tory of some of your household assets such as furniture, jewelry, computer
equipment, automobile, and so on. There are things in your home that
you probably never use that you can sell and raise some cash to pay off
part of your debt. Advertise these items in the newspaper, or have a giant
garage sale.

WOULD A PART TIME JOB HELP?

Q. *We have had unexpected medical expenses. Our income is not*
    enough to cover all the bills we have. I am considering getting a
    part-time job. My wife is working full time and we have three
    children. Would this be the smart thing to do?

Most people don't plan for unexpected emergencies and live from paycheck to paycheck.

Will getting a part-time job help? You need to determine if the amount
of extra income will be enough after calculating your travel time, cloth-
ing, food, and child care costs. If it ends up netting you very little income
after calculating your costs, don't do it.

It would be better if you could work overtime at your current job. If that isn't a possibility you might want to brush up on your skills by going back to school. You may be able to get a raise at your current employment or land a job with another company that offers you more money.

I had a client who went back to computer engineering school and ended up getting a new job that tripled his salary.

USE YOUR TALENT AND HOBBY
TO MAKE SOME MONEY

Q. *I want to earn extra money to pay off our bills. I am a home-maker with three children at home. Is there a way to make extra money from home?*

Absolutely! Most of us have special gifts and talents that we can make money with.

Make a list of the different things you like to do such as baking, crafts, sewing, art, music, and so on. With the list of things you enjoy doing, develop a plan to make money doing it. There are numerous books out on how to make money working from your home. Go to the library or bookstore and check them out.

My husband and I had a friend who enjoyed working on cars. He took an early retirement and during the interim of getting another job he worked on several individuals' cars and made money doing it. He was able to have a steady cash flow coming in to offset his bills, doing something he enjoyed.

HOLIDAY DEBT

Q. *I just received my credit card statement for all my holiday purchases. I blew it! I'm not sure if I can pay this off before the next holiday. Do you have any suggestions?*

Plan, plan, plan! Holiday credit card spending usually is never paid off by the next holiday. We all have a tendency to overspend; however, with a plan we don't have to go broke doing it.

As the holidays draw near, make a list of every purchase you think you will make. In your list include gifts, food, entertainment, clothes, baking ingredients, wrapping paper, tape, labels, ribbons, travel costs, and so on.

Review what you spent last year and set your budget. For example, let's say you spent $1,200 during the holiday season. If you divide that by 12 months the total would be $100. Now beginning in January you would need to set aside $100 per month to cover your holiday expenditures. Put the money in a savings account, or set up an automatic withdrawal from your paycheck to set the money aside. When the holidays come, you won't have to charge anything. You can pay cash and rid yourself of any new debt.

As for the remaining debt that you have from all the past holidays you never paid off, throw in extra money with your minimum payment and you'll get it paid off is less time.

CHAPTER 16

CREDIT REPAIR

Many individuals are either scared to see their credit reports because of past problems, or they are totally shocked at being turned down for credit because they never had past problems. Whatever the situation, it is important that you review your credit reports from all three credit reporting agencies—Experian (TRW), Trans Union, and Equifax—at least once a year, or prior to making any major purchase for credit. This will eliminate any surprises and allow you to correct any errors that are being reported. By correcting the inaccurate information being reported on your credit report prior to applying for credit, your chances of an approval are higher.

In a recent study the U.S. Public Interest Research Group found that nearly one-third of all consumer credit-bureau reports contain serious errors that could cause unfair denial of credit.

Among the findings:

- 29 percent of the credit reports contained serious errors, such as false delinquencies or accounts that did not belong to the consumer.
- 70 percent of the credit reports contained errors of some kind.
- 41 percent of the credit reports contained personal identifying information—such as an address—that was misspelled, outdated, belonged to a stranger, or was otherwise incorrect.
- 20 percent were missing important information that could demonstrate that a consumer was in fact creditworthy.
- 26 percent listed active credit accounts that had been closed by the consumer.

When you receive a copy of your credit report, review each entry on the report. (Listed separately from the entries on the credit report is a breakdown of the codes.) If, after reviewing your credit report, you find any items on your report that you feel are erroneous, inaccurate, incorrect, or incomplete, you can dispute the negative items on your report. The Fair Credit Reporting Act dictates that any dispute on a consumer credit report must be reinvestigated and removed if found to be inaccurate, unverifiable, or the creditor does not respond. The credit reporting agency will complete its investigation within 30 days of receiving your written dispute. If the creditor does not respond, the credit reporting agency must remove the negative entry from the report. If the creditor does respond and the item is not removed, the consumer can place a 100-word statement on any of the remaining items on the credit report explaining why this problem occurred. The statement will appear on the report every time a credit report is run. If you do not want to put a statement on the report, wait approximately 120 days from the updated credit report and try disputing again. Repeat the procedure as necessary.

Remember, the credit reporting agency must investigate the item with the creditor unless it feels it is irrelevant or frivolous.

INACCURATE INFORMATION

Q. *How does inaccurate information get on my credit report?*

A credit report is compiled by the credit reporting agencies. Each agency has subscribers who are the creditors you have accounts with presently or have had in the past.

Most creditors have their information computerized, which means there are operators who works for the creditor (not the credit reporting agency) who inputs your credit information into their computers. Many errors happen when the computer operators inputs inaccurate information. Frequently accounts that are paid off never get entered into the system. Bankruptcies are a common problem. Many accounts that were included in a bankruptcy are never corrected by the creditor and will show up on the credit report as still owed.

The credit reporting agencies are not the ones responsible for the inaccuracies. They only record what is given to them. It is important to review your credit reports yearly, or before you plan on establishing new credit for a home, car, or credit card.

You can challenge inaccurate entries on your credit report through the credit bureau that is reporting them. It must investigate inaccurate entries with the creditors. If the entries are unverifiable or incorrect, they must be removed.

It is advisable that you have a copy of your credit report from all three credit bureaus. When you write to them, include your full name, address, previous address, Social Security number, year of birth, and a copy of your driver's license or a statement with your name and address on it.

Trans Union
P.O. Box 390
Springfield, PA 19064

Equifax
P.O. Box 740193
Atlanta, GA 30374-0193

Experian
P.O. Box 2104
Allen, TX 75013

Experian (TRW), Trans Union, and Equifax charge $8 per credit report, unless you have been turned down for credit within the last 60 days. If you have been turned down for credit within the past 60 days you can receive your credit report free. Include the pertinent information of your identification and list the company who turned you down for credit.

A husband and wife must request their credit reports separately.

THE ITEM REAPPEARED AFTER I BOUGHT MY HOUSE

Q. *A few years ago I tried to refinance my home. There was a negative item on my credit report. The creditor issued a letter indicating it was an error. It went off my credit report, but it has since reappeared. What can I do?*

Any time you are getting a new mortgage or refinancing your home, the mortgage company will have a standard factual run on an individual or couple, which is a combination of the three credit bureaus, Experian (TRW), Trans Union, and Equifax. This is part of the qualification the underwriters will look for in approving a loan.

Frequently errors are found in these reports. If there are negative entries that have surfaced on these reports, the mortgage company will request a letter of explanation from you, or contact the creditor who is reporting this entry to verify if it is correct. If the entry is found to be incorrect, the creditor will submit a letter indicating the error and the entry will be corrected.

This will help gain an approval on a mortgage application, however the majority of the time the original credit bureaus have not been notified by the creditor, which is necessary to correct the entry in their systems. By not having it changed in their systems it can reappear on your credit report as a negative entry. Send a copy of the letter that was given to the mortgage company by the creditor with a letter to each credit bureau telling them to update their files.

It is always recommended to check your credit reports from all three bureaus before you apply for a mortgage or refinance. By doing this, you can solve any problems before you make an application and risk being denied credit.

CREDIT REPAIR COMPANIES

Q. *I have seen companies who advertise credit repair. What can these companies do to fix my credit report?*

Anytime a credit repair company guarantees that it can remove a negative entry from your credit report, watch out! Many credit repair companies charge an outrageous fee for their services. You are capable of repairing your own credit report.

The Fair Credit Reporting Act states that a consumer has the right to dispute inaccurate, incomplete, and erroneous information contained in his or her credit report. A credit repair company is writing these letters for you.

If there is inaccurate information on your credit report, write a letter to the credit bureau indicating what the inaccuracy is. The credit bureau must verify it with the creditor. If the creditor does not respond or the item is not verifiable, the inaccurate entry will be removed.

Many states have requirements that a credit repair company must follow to be in compliance with the law.

There are some reputable credit repair companies, but I recommend that you check out the company with the better business bureau to make sure there are no unresolved complaints on file. Many people are not comfortable working on their credit reports and will seek the assistance of a credit repair company.

A good resource on credit repair (in addition to *The Insiders Guide to Managing Your Credit*) is *The Credit Repair Kit* by John Ventura (Dearborn, 1998).

A NEW CREDIT FILE

Q. *I have heard of some companies who say they can get me a new credit file. Is this true?*

Creating a new credit file is called *file segregation*. What that means is that your Social Security number may be scrambled, your name altered, and address changed. This practice is illegal. I would never recommend file segregation to anyone.

Any company that represents to you that you can get a new credit file is breaking the law and you better not get involved with this deceit.

Several years ago I read an article in the newspaper about companies creating new credit files for individuals. The article stated that not only was the Internal Revenue Service looking for individuals who had changed their identities to obtain credit, but also the attorney general was looking for the companies who were following this practice.

Individuals who have gotten new credit files were individuals who were desperate to get credit because of past credit problems and were continuously denied new credit.

CORRECTING A BANKRUPTCY

Q. *Three years ago I filed for bankruptcy. I received a copy of my credit report and noticed that most of the accounts that were* *discharged through the bankruptcy are still showing collections and charge-offs. This is not correct. What can I do?*

Most of the credit reports that I have seen from individuals who have filed a bankruptcy have multiple errors. All the accounts that were discharged through the bankruptcy should be reported as discharged through bankruptcy. If the accounts are not being reported accurately, then you can dispute each of the accounts with the credit bureau. Review your credit report for all the inaccurate entries that you know were discharged through the bankruptcy. If they are still showing up as collections or charged-off accounts, obviously they were discharged through the bankruptcy and a letter should be sent to the credit reporting agency. The letter should state that you do not owe money on these accounts.

The credit reporting agency must investigate your dispute with the creditor. If the creditor does not respond, the entry will be removed. If the creditor does respond, a change in the entry should be noted that this account was part of the bankruptcy.

An account discharged through bankruptcy is better than a negative entry such as a charge-off or collection that has not been paid. The discharge brings closure to the account.

CHARGE-OFF ACCOUNT

Q. *I received a copy of my credit report and discovered three old accounts reporting a charge-off. I paid these accounts off. How can I get this corrected?*

A charge-off account means that the creditor gave up on you for any type of repayment. If you paid this account off, you can do one of two things.

First, write to the credit reporting agency and indicate in your letter that you do not have a charge-off account with this company and that you paid them in full. The credit reporting agency must investigate this with the creditor. The credit reporting agency has 30 days to respond to your letter with an updated credit report. If the creditor does not respond or the account is unverifiable, the entry will be removed from your credit report. If the creditor does respond, your credit report must be updated as to whatever the creditor states in its response. If the creditor continues to state that your account is unpaid, the entry will remain the same. If the creditor indicates that the account was paid, the entry may read "paid charge-off."

If you are not satisfied with what the creditor's response is, contact the creditor directly. If the creditor is indicating that you still have a balance, provide the creditor with a copy of your cancelled check so the records can be update.

TAX LIEN

Q. *I went to apply for a car loan. The car dealer ran a credit report on me and turned my application down because of a reported unpaid IRS tax lien. This IRS tax lien was paid off two years ago. What can I do to get this corrected on my credit report?*

Get a copy of your credit report from all three credit reporting agencies. Compare all three credit reports to see if all three have the tax lien reported and what the status is.

Because you already paid the tax lien off, you should have a copy of the release from the Internal Revenue Service. If you never received a copy of the release, contact the IRS and request a copy.

Once you receive a copy of the release, make three copies. Send a letter to all three credit reporting agencies with a copy of the tax release requesting that they update their records. Once the credit reporting agencies have updated their records, they will send you copies of the new credit reports with the changes.

Check with the county recorder to make sure the IRS recorded the tax release. If the IRS didn't, you must make sure that it is recorded showing the tax lien was paid; otherwise anytime you try to purchase or sell real estate, the tax lien will appear as unpaid.

Save your copy of the tax release from the IRS. You never know when you may need it in the future.

PAID JUDGMENT

Q. *There was a judgment filed against me last year. I paid it immediately. My credit report shows an unpaid judgment which is hurting me getting new credit. Is there anything I can do?*

Anytime a judgment is filed against an individual and the judgment was paid, the plaintiff who obtained the judgment must complete a paid satisfaction form and deliver it to the court within a certain time period. You need to contact the court where the judgment was granted to find out what amount of time is given for a paid satisfaction of judgment to be filed.

If the time period expired and the plaintiff never reported the paid judgment, then you can file a lawsuit against that party. You need to contact the court to see how much you can sue for.

I had a client who had a small claims judgment against him for $200. He paid the judgment immediately, however the plaintiff never reported the judgment as paid to the court.

My client sued the individual in small claims court for damaging his credit report by neglecting to report the paid account.

The party he was suing contacted my client prior to the court date. My client indicated that he would drop the case providing a "motion for relief from judgment by written stipulation" be filed. If the judge granted this stipulation, the judgment my client had against him would be dropped, and it would be as if he never had a judgment.

A "motion for relief from judgment by written stipulation" was granted to my client. He then dropped the pending lawsuit.

Once the paperwork was completed, my client sent a copy of the motion to all three credit reporting agencies. This resulted in all three credit reporting agencies deleting the judgment entry on his credit reports.

STUDENT LOAN

Q. *My student loan was turned over to a collection agency. I paid it off; however, it shows unpaid by Sallie Mae on my credit report. What can I do?*

You need to contact the collection agency to whom you paid the account. Explain your situation and find out why your account was never updated with Sallie Mae.

Have the collection agency mail you a letter stating that the account was paid off in full. Forward a copy of the letter to Sallie Mae for it to update your credit reports.

Request copies of your credit reports six weeks after you sent your letter to Sallie Mae to make sure the changes were made. If they weren't, contact Sallie Mae again and request a written letter from them indicating the account was paid. Once you get a copy of the letter, send a copy to all the credit reporting agencies to update their files. Once the credit report is updated, the credit reporting agency is required to send you a copy of the report at no additional charge.

WRONG SOCIAL SECURITY NUMBER

Q. *My credit report has a wrong Social Security number listed. There are also some accounts that are not mine. I have a common last name. Could my credit report be confused with someone else's?*

It is not uncommon to see someone with a common name have accounts that do not belong to them. Because your Social Security number is not accurate, you need to write to the credit reporting agency and correct the error. Identify the accounts that do not belong to you and request that they be removed.

There are times when a credit report is confused with someone else's, especially with someone with the same name.

This will happen frequently with a father and son with the same name.

When my husband and I were first married, we applied for a loan for an automobile. My husband's credit report showed three other car loans. My husband is a junior (Jr.) and his credit report was confused with my father-in-law's. There was no way we could have had three car loans at our young age.

The credit reporting agencies were notified of the errors; which were then corrected. All credit reports with my husband's name have a disclaimer from the credit reporting agency stating not to confuse the name with a family member's name.

I have seen this disclaimer on many of my client's credit reports when they have family members with the same name.

CHAPTER 17

REESTABLISHING CREDIT AFTER A BANKRUPTCY OR CREDIT PROBLEMS

Going through a bankruptcy or financial hardship could leave you with a sense of hopelessness about being able to qualify for credit in the future.

Bankruptcy doesn't carry the stigma it used to. With the past economic turmoil, more and more people were forced into bankruptcy. There are still others who opted not to file for bankruptcy and tried to hang on. Whatever the case may be, their credit reports have been ruined.

With so many people going through hard times, lenders and other institutions have created programs to help individuals reestablish themselves in the world of credit.

Lenders see you as being a higher risk, which results in higher interest rates and lower lines of credit. Many people will balk at paying the higher rates; however, unless you are willing to wait seven to ten years to have all the negative information dropped from your credit report, you need to start somewhere.

There are subprime lenders who will make loans, to people with past credit problems. There are automobile dealers who will help those with past credit problems purchase or lease an automobile. There are credit card companies who offer secured credit cards and a few credit card companies who will offer you an unsecured credit card if you have had no credit problems within six months of your application.

Once you have established good credit for at least two years with no delinquencies, try to refinance your home or car to get a lower interest rate. Also with credit cards, you can try to qualify for a lower interest rate card and pay your higher interest rate card off.

The interesting thing about qualifying for credit after a bankruptcy or a financial hardship is it is easier to be approved to get a mortgage and automobile rather than a credit card. The difference between the two is that a home mortgage and automobile loan are secured by the properties, and a credit card is unsecured.

There is always a way to reestablish yourself after hardship. It just takes time and patience.

The main thing to remember is to never pay any of your bills late where a negative mark would be entered on your credit report after your bankruptcy or past credit problems. It will automatically disqualify you for any new credit.

ANGELA'S STORY

Angela had a messy divorce which left her credit report in shambles. She was determined to try and pick up the pieces of her life and reestablish new credit in her own name.

When Angela called my office she told me she wanted to get her credit report cleared of all the inaccuracies being reported. Her goal was to rebuild her credit and purchase a house.

The first thing I did was have Angela request copies of her credit report. Most of the entries on the credit report were her ex-husband's accounts and had a negative rating.

She sent letters to the credit reporting agencies disputing all the inaccurate accounts. I instructed Angela to get two secured credit cards and establish a good payment pattern, which would be reflected on her credit report.

About ten months after Angela had begun reestablishing her credit, she called to let me know that she was making her final payment on her automobile. She was so excited because all her payments had been on time and she knew that the entry would look good when trying to qualify for a home loan.

Angela had never mentioned anything to me about her car loan. I went back and reviewed her credit report and discovered the company who financed her car never reported any payments. I asked Angela about this and she telephoned the loan company. Evidently the loan company did not subscribe to any of the credit reporting agencies. The past three years that Angela thought she was rebuilding her credit history on her credit report was for nothing.

I explained to Angela that in order to rebuild her credit report with positive credit history she needed to show the car payments being made.

Angela's car was an older model and needed repairs. She was devastated.

I introduced Angela to an auto specialist who was able to help her get into a new car. The loan company that he matched Angela with reported to all three of the credit reporting agencies.

Angela couldn't have been happier. She had a new car and was able to establish a good payment history with the loan company. Her accounts with both the secured credit card companies also were reported as an excellent rating. Her dream of buying a home was on its way to becoming a reality.

By waiting and rebuilding her credit, Angela will be in a position to purchase a home within two years of establishing her new credit.

REESTABLISHING CREDIT AFTER TWO YEARS

Q. *Two years ago I was forced to file for a bankruptcy because my business failed. What can I do to reestablish myself?*

Reestablishing credit after a bankruptcy can take some time. It is not an overnight process.

If you were unable to keep one or two of your credit cards after your bankruptcy, getting a secured credit card would be a good beginning. There are banks who offer a VISA or MasterCard if you secure it with a deposit at their banks. Check with your local bank to see if a secured credit card program is available. When you get your secured credit card, make small purchases and pay the purchases off with each statement. This will show a good payment history.

A cosigner for a loan may help you in reestablishing credit. A friend or relative can request a user credit card in your name on her or his credit card to show a line of credit for you.

Car dealers have special deals for individuals who have filed bankruptcy. Be prepared to pay a large deposit and a high interest rate.

Once you have established new credit after your bankruptcy, make sure you have a budget set so you do not fall into the same trap as before. It could take two years before you are able to get credit easily.

PURCHASING A HOME

Q. *We were doing great financially. My husband was making a good income. Our credit card payments were $900 per month. He was laid off his job and later diagnosed with a brain tumor. We could not pay our bills. We went to Consumer Credit Counseling Service but our situation was too bad for them to help. We filed for bankruptcy. We are now trying to put our lives back together. One day we want to buy a home. Is this possible?*

Yes, it is possible, however you must wait at least two years before you could possibly qualify for a new mortgage. There are a few lenders who will give you a home loan prior to the two years; however you would have to go through a mortgage broker who has access to different lenders offering these programs.

The lender will want to see two to three new open accounts with a good payment pattern since the bankruptcy or credit problems.

There is a question in the loan application for a mortgage that will ask you if you have ever filed for a bankruptcy. It is important that you inform the loan officer about your situation before you apply. A bankruptcy is a public notice, so if for some reason it is not on your credit report, it is filed at the county recorder's office, and it could easily be revealed. Have the lender prequalify you before you look for a home.

The lender is looking for several things in qualification. They want to see that you have been able to reestablish good credit since your bankruptcy. Job stability, income, and your down payment will play an important role in your qualification.

Another way to purchase a home would be to assume someone else's FHA or VA loan. If you have the money to assume the loan, there would be no qualification. You would not have to wait any length of time to assume someone else's loan. That is always the best way to purchase, especially if you have had a bankruptcy.

PROBLEMS GETTING EMPLOYMENT

Q. *I filed for a bankruptcy and am now unemployed. Whenever I have applied for employment, once the company I have interviewed with runs a credit report on me they won't hire me. What can I do?*

It is important that you realize that when you are completing and signing an employment application that there may be a section authorizing the employer to run a credit report. If you see this authorization on the application it is important that you disclose to the potential employer about your past bankruptcy and inquire what type of background check they will be conducting.

Prior to hiring an employee, if the employer indicates that there are certain policies and guidelines the company enforces, and that a past bankruptcy would disqualify the potential candidate, don't bother going any further. By turning in an application knowing that it will be rejected, you are risking excessive inquiries on your record. Also, any inquiry made by a potential employer would be notated on the credit report for others to view. You may not want another employer to see where you have applied for employment prior to their company.

By being up front about your past bankruptcy with the employer, possibly a decision could be made without running a credit report.

SECURED CREDIT CARD COMPANIES

Q. *I heard that a secured credit card is a good way to go after going through financial problems. Is this true?*

Yes! But a secured credit card is a good way to reestablish credit only if you make your payments on time, or preferably pay off your balance in full every month. The main purpose for getting a secured credit card is to show a good payment pattern on your credit report.

After you have had the credit card for at least two years and show a good payment history, apply for an unsecured credit card with a lower interest rate.

The interest rate on a secured credit card is usually high, and there is usually an annual fee plus a one-time set up fee.

UNSECURED CREDIT CARD OFFERS EVEN WITH PAST PROBLEMS

Q. *I am getting offers for an unsecured credit card. The application says I can get one even with a past bankruptcy. What is the catch? How does this program work?*

There are companies now offering unsecured credit cards to individuals who have experienced past credit problems or a bankruptcy.

The interest rates are high, the annual fee is high, the set-up charge is high, the limits are low, and there usually is no grace period with the interest.

These credit cards can help you reestablish your credit, but read the small print on the application. Once you are reestablished, close the account and get a better low interest credit card.

STORE CREDIT CARDS

Q. *Can I get a store credit card with a past bankruptcy?*

Sometimes, if you explain your situation to your local merchants, they may have special programs available to you. The merchant may require a large deposit, and a high interest rate. The most important thing to find out is if the merchant reports payment history to a credit reporting agency. If they do, make your payments on time, and pay the account off as soon as possible. You are only trying to improve your credit rating. If the merchant doesn't report to a credit reporting agency, try another merchant. Don't get credit with any merchant unless it is a subscriber to a credit reporting agency and reports your payment pattern monthly.

AUTOMOBILES

Q. *I need a new car. Three years ago I had severe credit problems but have since paid off my old debts. My credit report looks bad. Where can I get a car without paying an exorbitant interest rate?*

After going through past credit problems you need to realize that most banks who work with the car dealers will consider you a high risk.

Sometimes it is easier to lease a car rather than purchase one. If you find a dealer that will lease a car to you, it probably will offer you a two-year lease. If you can afford it, take it. The reason you want to take advantage of the two-year lease is to demonstrate that you will make all the payments on time and establish a good payment pattern.

Once the lease is up, you will be in a better position to get another car and you would have improved your credit report.

If you have had a repossession of a vehicle and it is reported on your credit report, it is more difficult to get into another car loan.

There are some dealers who specialize in individuals who have had a bankruptcy or problems with their credit, including repossessions. Be prepared to pay a large deposit and high interest rate. If you have paid your account on time, after 24 months you may be able to have your bank or credit union refinance the car at a lower interest rate. Be sure to make your payments on time to build up your credit report. Be sure your payments are reported to the credit reporting agencies.

PAY OFF OLD BILLS THAT WERE DISCHARGED

Q. *I went through a bankruptcy several years ago. All my accounts were discharged. I want to go back now and pay them off. Will this help me get new credit?*

If you went back and paid off all your debts that were discharged through the bankruptcy, it may or may not help you get new credit. It depends on what type of credit you were trying to get.

I would suggest that if you do pay off the debts that were discharged, that you make an agreement with the creditor to remove the entry from your credit report or report that it is paid in full. If the creditor will not make any changes on your credit report, get a letter from them stating that the account was paid off.

You will be more likely to get a home loan and automobile with possibly better interest rates if you paid your past debts off. Trying to get a credit card could be more difficult.

When you get a home or automobile loan, you usually have a sales representative who you can explain your situation to and provide the appropriate documents to boost your chances of qualifying for a loan with the best rates. On the other hand, when you apply for a credit card there is no representative to help you. There is only an application that is turned in and a credit report that is run, not giving you the opportunity to explain your situation.

Many people fight having to file for bankruptcy and feel guilty doing it. With a bankruptcy, the court forgives the debt, which is reported as discharged. It is important that you forgive yourself and not fall into the same problems which caused you to go bankrupt.

Because all your debts were discharged through the bankruptcy, you are under no legal obligation to go back and pay the debts off. Only do this if you feel it is right for you and perhaps your conscience.

CHAPTER 18

MISCELLANEOUS QUESTIONS

75-YEAR-OLD RAN UP THE CREDIT CARDS

Q. *My 75-year-old mother ran up $60,000 in credit card bills. She has been trying to hide it from me, but the creditors are calling me to collect. The creditors don't have her address or telephone number. All the bills and calls are coming to my house. She owns three homes and has no equity. Her income is too low to pay these credit cards off. I think she should file for a bankruptcy but she doesn't want to. She's fighting me on this. I'm at my wits end. Should she file for bankruptcy?*

The first thing you need to do is back off your mother. Remember, mom is always mom who wants to feel she is in charge of her life. The more you push her, the more she will resist your help.

For your mother to file for bankruptcy at her age is not a necessity. She has already quit making the payments, and will no longer be able to use her credit cards. Because the letters and telephone calls are not going directly to her she will not have to endure any harassment.

One remedy the creditor has to collect is to file a lawsuit against her. As she barely has an income and no equity in her houses, it would be tough for the creditors to collect.

When the creditors assess her financial situation as well as her age, they will probably back away from her and charge off the accounts.

Because your mother is uncomfortable filing for bankruptcy, analyze how much of a payment she can make on each credit card. For example, it may be only $10 per month per credit card. Whatever the amount is, help your mother write a letter to each of the creditors explaining her financial situation. Make the offer to pay $10 per month, with no more interest or fees being added. If the creditors agree to this arrangement, have them put it in writing and begin making the payments.

Your mother may feel better knowing she is paying at least something towards the bill.

Let's hope mom learned her lesson.

SCAM ARTIST TOOK ADVANTAGE OF FATHER

Q. *My 78-year-old widowered father fell prey to some scam artists who came to his home to repair his driveway. They befriended him, and before long convinced him to advance them cash for the driveway repairs that never happened.*

As the weeks went by, these scam artists kept reappearing at my father's house. He kept paying them cash for other repairs they promised to do. One day they convinced him to go to a department store and charge $15,000 worth of jewelry. Another time they convinced him to charge tires for their truck. Eventually $45,000 was run up in credit card purchases. The scam artists disappeared with all the purchases my father made.

Obviously he was not in his right mind or this wouldn't have happened. Is he liable for these charges?

Nothing is more disheartening than hearing stories of elderly people being taken advantage of from scam artists with one thing in mind—to rip the elderly off.

Unfortunately your father could be liable for the repayment of the purchases. I would suggest that your father go to an attorney and have an attorney prepare a letter on your father's behalf explaining the situation. Perhaps he could suggest a compromise or settlement that the creditors may accept. The creditors also may take pity on the situation and waive the charges. It is worth a try.

I'm sure your father is embarrassed about the situation and didn't know how to get out of it. Being direct and up front with the creditors is your best chance of solving this problem.

DEFERRED PAYMENTS FOR SIX MONTHS

Q. *I have seen advertisements offering merchandise you can pur-chase with payments deferred for up to six months. Is this a good way to go?*

Deferred payment programs are enticements for you to make purchases. Always read the fine print. With deferred payments you may be charged interest during the six months that is deferred. You would owe more money on the balance when you begin making your payments because of the interest charges.

Also, if you violate any provision in the contract, the whole balance could become due. If you are late in making your first payment, additional fees could result.

Every company has its own policy on deferred programs. Make sure you understand what you are getting into before making any commitments.

CREDIT CARD OR DEBIT CARD

Q. *Now that the banks have debit cards for VISA and MasterCard, which is the best way to purchase—using my credit card or debit card?*

There are different uses for each of the cards. With your credit card you create a bill and the debit card automatically pays a bill by deducting funds from your bank account. The credit card has no connection with your bank accounts.

There are three reasons to use your credit card.

1. Your credit card account is not immediately debited. If you have a grace period with your account, you would have approximately 25 to 30 days to pay the charge with no interest. With the debit card your account is immediately affected.
2. You have more leverage with a credit card than with a debit card in settling disputes about purchases.
3. The liability for loss or theft is less on a credit card than on a debit card.

On the other side, the debit cards are often substituted for cash. They are more often compared with checks than with credit cards. When you use your debit card, proper point of sale or point of purchase equipment must be available to electronically transmit the information on your card to the bank. It also credits the merchant's account immediately with the amount of the sale.

The debit card is not reported on your credit report. Your payment activity on your credit card will be reported monthly.

CUT-UP YOUR CARD AND RETURN IT

Q. *I paid off my credit card and cut it up and threw it in the trash. The credit card company sent me a bill for an annual fee of $25. I threw the statement away because I was no longer using the card.*

When I received a copy of my credit report, the credit card company had a $25 balance and charged off my account, leaving a negative mark. I don't feel I owe this because I no longer have the card. What can I do?

Never assume that your credit card account is closed unless you mail the credit card company your cut-up cards, requesting that your account be permanently closed.

Not using your credit card does not automatically close your account. If the terms of your agreement include an annual fee, it must be paid unless you canceled the card. The annual fee is usually added onto your credit card balance.

When you continuously ignored the statements, the credit card company eventually charged off your account.

Contact the credit card company and explain your misunderstanding of the annual fee. Explain that you cut the credit card up and threw it in the trash thinking that was all you needed to do to cancel the account. Note that there has been no activity.

Make a written arrangement with a supervisor to pay the $25 fee with the understanding that the account is closed and that the credit card company will remove the derogatory entry from your credit report. The credit card company is under no obligation to remove this, however speak to a supervisor about your situation and see if something can be worked out. If it refuses to remove the derogatory remark, you have two choices. Attach a statement to your credit report (the agency *must* allow you to do this), or pay the $25 and make sure the account is reported paid in full, even if the charge-off still appears.

CHECKING ACCOUNT DENIED

Q. *I went to open a checking account and was denied. Does a bank report checking and savings accounts on your credit report? Why would I be denied opening an account?*

Banks and savings and loans have their own internal reporting system that is reported to other banks and institutions. It is called Chex System. This information is not reported to credit reporting agencies.

If you have had a checking account closed because of your account being overdrawn and money is still owed to the bank, any bank that belongs to the Chex System will deny you opening a new account. When you are completing the paperwork in getting a new account, your name and Social Security number will be input into the bank's system. If you are on the Chex System with a past problem on any account, you will be denied.

The best way to handle this situation is to find out what the problem is and which bank is reporting you.

Contact the bank and find out why you are being reported. If you owe the bank money, pay it off so you can open a new account. See if the bank will remove your name from the system once you have paid your account off.

BAD CHECK

Q. *Recently I was shopping at a store and wrote a check for my purchase. The store turned my check down and said I was being reported by Telecheck. They gave me a telephone number to call. It appears there was a bad check for $15 that was never cleared. Does this show up on my credit report?*

There are companies that many merchants contract with to protect the merchant from individuals who write bad checks. If you have an unpaid check that was written to a store that subscribes to one of these services, your name, account number of your check, and your driver's license number are input into the system. If you go to another store that subscribes to the same service and you try to purchase by check, when the clerk inputs your driver's license or checking account number into the cash register, your purchase will be denied. The merchant will give you the name and telephone number of the company that is refusing the cashing of your check.

When the company receives the check you wrote for insufficient funds, the company will send you a letter requesting the amount of the check plus additional fees. Once you have paid the company by cashier's check or money order, your name will be deleted from its records and you will no longer have problems writing checks.

The companies who service the merchants with these bad check reports do not report you to the credit reporting agencies. The only time you will be reported to a credit reporting agency is when you refuse to pay the check and the company handling the check turns it over to a collection agency. The collection agency will then report you to the credit reporting agencies.

If the merchant is handling its own collection of a bad check and the merchant is not part of a check servicing company, your name is not reported on any system. It is against the law to write bad checks and the merchant, after several attempts to collect, may elect to sue you. The merchant also may turn your check over to a collection agency, which will report you to the credit reporting agencies.

CONSUMER CREDIT COUNSELING SERVICE ON MY CREDIT REPORT

Q. *I went to Consumer Credit Counseling Service because I wanted to manage my bills better. None of my accounts were paid late but I wanted to make one payment to CCCS and have them pay my accounts. I went to refinance my house and was turned down because CCCS was noted on my accounts. What is the problem? My credit rating is excellent.*

Consumer Credit Counseling Service is a good company to use if you are having problems paying your bills. Many times CCCS can negotiate with the creditors to reduce your interest and payments.

The downside to this is that any creditors that CCCS pays or negotiates with on behalf of its clients, has the option to report this on your credit report. Unfortunately, a notation that CCCS is assisting you with your payments can be viewed as a negative entry on your credit report.

When a lender is looking at your application for a refinance of your home, the credit entries that are noted with CCCS are viewed as bad as a bankruptcy. You will not be able to qualify for a loan offering the best rates.

A subprime lender may assist you with your refinance; however, you may not want to pay the higher rates.

My suggestion to you would be to cancel your arrangement with CCCS and contact all your creditors letting them know that you are taking over the payments of your accounts. See if the creditors will remove the entry stating CCCS from your credit report. If the creditors remove the entries and your credit report has no problems listed, you should be able to reapply for your refinance.

MY CREDIT CARD STATEMENT SAYS
I CAN SKIP A PAYMENT

Q. *On several occasions my credit card statement will indicate that I can skip the monthly payment for that month. Is this a good idea?*

No! Never skip your monthly payment, even if the credit card company tells you that you can. Though you skip your monthly payment, the interest doesn't stop and your balance increases.

Whenever a payment is skipped, the grace period that is allowing you to pay off your balance without interest becomes void. By losing the grace period and paying additional interest for the second month, an 18 percent interest rate rises to 26 percent on the final balance.

The only winner when you skip your payment is the credit card company.

DELINQUENT ACCOUNT SOLD THREE TIMES

Q. *I had an account that was delinquent and eventually charged off.*
The company sold my account to another company which was
listed on my credit report. The second company turned around
and sold it to a third company and is also reporting this on my
credit report. Do the three entries make the report look worse?

It is not uncommon for an original lender to sell the bad debt to an outside company after it is charged off. You can see the account listed on your
credit report as being unpaid and transferred to other companies.

Each time it is the same debt being reported on your credit report and
it should not be counted against you again.

No matter how many times the account is sold, the original date of last
activity or payment on the account is what is measured for it to drop off
the credit report. For example, if you had an account that was charged off
in February 1992, the seven years would begin. In February 1999 the item
will automatically be removed from the credit report.

It doesn't matter how many times the creditor sells the account after the
charge-off, the date of last activity is not reset.

Most bad debts, as well as good credit history, will be removed from
your credit report seven years after the date of the last activity. Bankruptcies can remain for up to ten years from the date of filing.

STUDENT LOAN SOLD THREE TIMES

Q. *I took out a student loan. The bank sold the loan to another*
bank. This happened three times. I continued making my
payments but they were sent back to me indicating the account
was sold. After three months I finally received a statement.
The new lender indicated that I owed three payments. Now my
credit report says I paid late. What can I do?

Hopefully you saved the letters that the bank sent you refusing your
payment because the loan was sold.

If you can find the letters and checks, make a copy of each and mail them certified mail with a return receipt to the new lender. In your letter request that the new lender update its records and remove the late payment entry from your credit report.

The bank should remove the negative entry off your credit report. If you are having problems getting the bank to agree to this, speak to a manager or supervisor. It wasn't your fault the bank sold the loan and your payments crossed over.

When you have cleared up the matter, have the bank send you a letter stating its error and that it will be removing its negative entry from your credit report.

Request a copy of your credit report six weeks after the bank agrees to correct its files. If the credit report has not been changed then, make a copy of the letter from the bank and attach it to a letter to the credit reporting agencies requesting they update their records. You should receive an updated credit report within 45 days of your letter.

EPILOGUE

As you have concluded from reading this book, you may have discovered situations similar to the problems you have encountered in the past or are presently facing.

By reading all the different scenarios and problems other individuals have had, I hope that you were able to discover answers and solutions for your particular situation.

As the years go by, your financial situation will change—hopefully for the better. The important thing to remember with any situation—whether it be good or bad—is that you don't repeat the same mistakes. It is important that you learn from the past and educate yourself on all areas of credit and finance. This book can be used as a resource book in your library for future situations that may occur.

Teach your children about money, credit, and finances at an early age. Show them how to budget and manage their money. You could be preventing them from creating unnecessary financial hardships in their adult lives.

Your children will respond to money and credit the same way you do. If you find you are going through tough times, the way you handle the situation will be an example to your children.

Use whatever experience you have had to further your growth in the world of credit. Knowing the things that you do now should prevent you from falling into future problems.

Try not to get discouraged. Develop a plan. Never give up your hope or faith, because there is always an answer and a solution.

APPENDIX: STATE AND LOCAL CONSUMER PROTECTION AGENCIES

Usually the government agencies most responsive to our needs are those at the local and state level. These agencies have a better understanding of the needs of the people in their area. Following is a list of state and local government protection agencies that can provide assistance in understanding your rights and helping you enforce them.

Alabama

State Office

Consumer Affairs Division
Office of the Attorney General
11 S. Union St.
Montgomery, AL 36130
334-242-7334
800-392-5658 (toll-free in AL)

Alaska

The Consumer Protection Section in the Office of the Attorney General has been closed. Consumers with complaints are being referred to the better business bureau, small claims court, and private attorneys.

Arizona

State Offices

Consumer Protection
Office of the Attorney General
1275 W. Washington St., Rm. 259
Phoenix, AZ 85007

602-542-3702
602-542-5763 (consumer information and complaints)
800-352-8431 (toll-free in AZ)
TDD: 602-542-5002

Assistant Attorney General
Consumer Protection
Office of the Attorney General
402 W. Congress South Building., Ste. 315
Tucson, AZ 85701
602-628-6504

County Offices

Apache County Attorney's Office
PO Box 637
St. Johns, AZ 85936
520-337-4364, ext. 240

Cochise County Attorney's Office
PO Drawer CA
Bisbee, AZ 85603
520-432-9377

Coconino County Attorney's Office
Coconino County Courthouse
100 E. Birch
Flagstaff, AZ 86001
520-779-6518

Gila County Attorney's Office
1400 E. Ash St.
Globe, AZ 85501
520-425-3231

Graham County Attorney's Office
Graham County Courthouse
800 W. Main
Safford, AZ 85546
520-428-3620

Greenlee County Attorney's Office
PO Box 1717
Clifton, AZ 85533
520-865-4108

LaPaz County Attorney's Office
1320 Kofa Ave.
PO Box 709
Parker, AZ 85344
520-669-6118

Mohave County Attorney's Office
315 N. 4th St.
PO Box 7000
Kingman, AZ 86402-7000
520-753-0719

Navajo County Attorney's Office
PO Box 668
Holbrook, AZ 86025
520-524-4026

Pima County Attorney's Office
1400 Great American Tower
32 N. Stone
Tucson, AZ 85701
520-740-5733

Pinal County Attorney's Office
PO Box 887
Florence, AZ 85232
520-868-6271

Santa Cruz County Attorney's Office
2100 N. Congress Dr., Ste. 201
Nogales, AZ 85621
520-287-2468

Yavapai County Attorney's Office
Yavapai County Courthouse
Prescott, AZ 86301
520-771-3344

Yuma County Attorney's Office
168 S. Second Ave.
Yuma, AZ 85364
520-329-2270

City Office

Deputy City Attorney
Consumer Affairs Division
Tucson City Attorney's Office
110 E. Pennington St., 2nd Fl.
PO Box 27210
Tucson, AZ 85726-7210
520-791-4886

Arkansas

State Office

Director, Consumer Protection Division
Office of the Attorney General
200 Catlett Prien
323 Center St.
Little Rock, AR 72201
501-682-2341
TDD: 501-682-2014
800-482-8982 (toll-free voice/TDD in AR)

California

State Offices

Director, California Dept. of Consumer Affairs
400 R St., Ste. 3000
Sacramento, CA 95814
916-445-1254 (consumer information)
916-322-1700 (TDD)
800-952-5200 (toll-free in CA)

Bureau of Automotive Repair
California Dept. of Consumer Affairs
10240 Systems Pkwy.
Sacramento, CA 95827
916-445-1254
TDD: 916-322-1700
800-952-5210 (toll-free in CA, auto repair
   only)

Office of the Attorney General
Public Inquiry Unit
PO Box 944255
Sacramento, CA 94244-2550
916-322-3360
TDD: 916-324-5564
800-952-5225 (toll-free in CA)

County Offices

Commissioner, Alameda County
   Consumer Affairs Commission
4400 MacArthur Blvd.
Oakland, CA 94619
510-535-6444

District Attorney
Contra Costa County District Attorney's
   Office
725 Court St., 4th Fl.
PO Box 670
Martinez, CA 94553
510-646-4500

Senior Deputy District Attorney
Business Affairs Unit
Fresno County District Attorney's Office
1250 Van Ness Ave., 2nd Fl.
Fresno, CA 93721
209-488-3156

District Attorney
Criminal Section
Kern County District Attorney's Office
1215 Truxtun Ave., 4th Fl.
Bakersfield, CA 93301
805-861-2421

Director, Los Angeles County Dept. of
   Consumer Affairs
500 W. Temple St., Rm. B-96
Los Angeles, CA 90012
213-974-1452 (public)

Director, Citizens Service Office
Marin County Mediation Services
4 Mount Lassen Dr.
San Rafael, CA 94903
415-499-7454

Deputy District Attorney
Consumer Protection Division
Marin County District Attorney's Office
Hall of Justice, Rm. 183
San Rafael, CA 94903
415-499-6450

District Attorney
Mendocino County District Attorney's Office
PO Box 1000
Ukiah, CA 95482
707-463-4211

Monterey County District Attorney
Consumer Protection Division
PO Box 1369
Salinas, CA 93902
408-755-5073

Deputy District Attorney
Consumer Affairs Division
Napa County District Attorney's Office
931 Parkway Mall
PO Box 720
Napa, CA 94559
707-253-4211

Supervising District Attorney
Consumer/Environmental Protection Unit
Orange County District Attorney's Office
405 West 5th Street, Ste. 606
Santa Ana, CA 92701
714-568-1240

Deputy District Attorney
Economic Crime Division
Riverside County District Attorney's Office
4075 Main St.
Riverside, CA 92501
909-275-5400

Supervising Deputy District Attorney
Consumer and Environmental Protection
   Division
Sacramento County District Attorney's Office
PO Box 749
Sacramento, CA 95812-0749
916-440-6174

Director, Consumer Fraud Division
San Diego County District Attorney's
    Office
PO Box X-1011
San Diego, CA 92112-4192
619-531-3507 (fraud complaint line)

Consumer Protection Unit
San Francisco County District Attorney's
    Office
732 Brannan St.
San Francisco, CA 94103
415-552-6400 (public inquiries)
415-553-1814 (complaints)

Consumer Mediator
San Joaquin County District Attorney's
    Office
222 E. Weber, Rm. 412
PO Box 990
Stockton, CA 95202
209-468-2481

Director, Economic Crime Unit
Consumer Fraud Dept.
County Government Center
1050 Monterey St., Rm. 235
San Luis Obispo, CA 93408
805-781-5856

Deputy in Charge
Consumer Fraud and Environmental
    Protection Unit
San Mateo County District Attorney's
    Office
401 Marshall St.
Hall of Justice and Records
Redwood City, CA 94063
415-363-4656

Deputy District Attorney
Consumer Protection Unit
Santa Barbara County District Attorney's
    Office
1105 Santa Barbara St.
Santa Barbara, CA 93101
805-568-2300

Deputy District Attorney
Consumer Fraud Unit
Santa Clara County District Attorney's Office
70 W. Hedding St., West Wing
San Jose, CA 95110
408-299-8478

Coordinator, Santa Clara County
    Consumer Protection Unit
70 West Hedding St., West Wing, Lower
    Level
San Jose, CA 95110-1705
408-299-4211

Coordinator, Division of Consumer Affairs
Santa Cruz County District Attorney's Office
701 Ocean St., Rm. 200
Santa Cruz, CA 95060
408-454-2050

Deputy District Attorney
Consumer Affairs Unit
Solano County District Attorney's Office
600 Union Ave.
Fairfield, CA 94533
707-421-6860

Deputy District Attorney
Consumer Fraud Unit
Stanislaus County District Attorney's Office
PO Box 442
Modesto, CA 95353-0442
209-525-5550

Deputy District Attorney
Consumer Affairs Unit
600 Union Ave.
Fairfield, CA 94533
707-421-6860

Deputy District Attorney
Consumer and Environmental Protection
    Division
Ventura County District Attorney's Office
800 S. Victoria Ave.
Ventura, CA 93009
805-654-3110

Supervising Deputy District Attorney
Special Services Unit
Consumer/Environmental
Yolo County District Attorney's Office
PO Box 245
Woodland, CA 95776
916-666-8424

City Offices

Chief Deputy District Attorney
Special Services Unit
Consumer/Envirnomental
Yolo County District Attorney's Office
PO Box 245
Woodland, CA 95776
916-666-8424

Supervising Deputy City Attorney
Consumer Protection Division
Los Angeles City Attorney's Office
200 N. Main St.
1600 City Hall East
Los Angeles, CA 90012
213-485-4515

Consumer Affairs Specialist
Consumer Protection, Fair Housing and
    Public Rights Unit
1685 Main St., Rm. 310
Santa Monica, CA 90401
310-458-8336
310-458-8370 (Spanish hotline)

Colorado

State Office

Consumer Protection Unit
Office of the Attorney General
1525 Sherman St., 5th Floor
Denver, CO 80203-1760
303-866-5189

County Offices

District Attorney
Archuleta, LaPlata, and San Juan Counties
District Attorney's Office
PO Drawer 3455
Durango, CO 81302
970-247-8850

District Attorney
Boulder County District Attorney's Office
PO Box 471
Boulder, CO 80306
303-441-3700

Chief
Denver District Attorney's Consumer
    Economic Crimes Division
303 W. Colfax Ave., Ste. 1300
Denver, CO 80204
303-640-5956 (administration)
303-640-3557 (complaints)

Chief Deputy District Attorney
Economic Crime Division
El Paso and Teller Counties District
    Attorney's Office
105 E. Vermijo, Ste. 205
Colorado Springs, CO 80903-2083
719-520-6002

District Attorney
Pueblo County District Attorney's Office
210 W. 8th Street, Ste. 801
Pueblo, CO 81003
719-583-6030

Chief Investigator
Weld County District Attorney's
    Consumer Office
PO Box 1167
Greeley, CO 80632
970-356-4010

Connecticut

State Offices

Commissioner, Dept. of Consumer
    Protection
165 Capitol Ave.
Hartford, CT 06106
860-566-2534
800-842-2649 (toll-free in CT)

Assistant Attorney General
Antitrust/Consumer Protection
Office of Attorney General
110 Sherman St.
Hartford, CT 06015
860-566-5374

City Office

Director, Middletown Office of Consumer
    Protection
City Hall
245 DeKoven Dr.
PO Box 1300
Middletown, CT 06457
860-344-3491
TDD: 860-344-3521

Delaware

State Offices

Director, Consumer Protection Unit
Department of Justice
820 N. French St.
Wilmington, DE 19801
302-577-3250

Deputy Attorney General
Fraud and Consumer Protection Unit
Office of the Attorney General
820 N. French St.
Wilmington, DE 19801
302-577-2500

District of Columbia

Director, Dept. of Consumer and
    Regulatory Affairs
614 H St., NW
Washington, DC 20001
202-727-7120

Florida

State Offices

Director, Dept. of Agriculture and
    Consumer Services
Division of Consumer Services
407 South Calhoun St.
Mayo Bldg., 2nd Floor
Tallahassee, FL 32399-0800
904-488-2221
800-435-7352 (toll-free in FL)

Chief, Consumer Litigation Section
110 S.E. 6th St.
Fort Lauderdale, FL 33301
954-712-4600

Assistant Deputy Attorney General
Economic Crimes Division
Office of the Attorney General
110 S.E. 6th St.
Fort Lauderdale, FL 33301
954-712-4600

County Offices

Director, Broward County Consumer
    Affairs Division
115 S. Andrews Ave.
Annex Room A460
Fort Lauderdale, FL 33301
305-765-5355

Consumer Advocate
Metropolitan Dade County
Consumer Protection Division
140 W. Flagler St., Ste. 902
Miami, FL 33130
305-375-4222

Chief, Dade County Economic Crime Unit
Office of the State's Attorney
1350 N.W. 12th Ave., 5th Floor
Graham Building
Miami, FL 33136-2111
305-547-0671

Director, Hillsborough County Commerce
Dept.
Consumer Protection Unit
PO Box 1110
Tampa, FL 33601
813-272-6750

Chief, Orange County Consumer Fraud
Unit
250 N. Orange Ave.
PO Box 1673
Orlando, FL 32802
407-836-2490

Citizens Intake
Office of the State's Attorney
401 N. Dixie Highway, Ste. 1600
West Palm Beach, FL 33401
407-355-7108

Director, Palm Beach County Division of
Consumer Affairs
50 S. Military Tr., Ste. 201
West Palm Beach, FL 33415
561-233-4820

Consumer Affairs/Code Compliance
Manager
7530 Little Rd., Ste. 140
New Port Richey, FL 34654
813-847-8110

Director, Pinellas County Office of
Consumer Protection
PO Box 17268
Clearwater, FL 34622-0268
813-464-6219

City Offices

Chief of Consumer Affairs
City of Jacksonville
Division of Consumer Affairs
421 W. Church St., Ste. 404
Jacksonville, FL 32202
904-630-3667

Department Secretary
Lauderhill Consumer Protection Board
1176 N.W. 42nd Way
Lauderhill, FL 33313
954-321-2456

Georgia

State Office

Administrator
Governor's Office of Consumer Affairs
2 Martin Luther King, Jr. Dr., S.E., Ste.
356
Atlanta, GA 30334
404-656-3790
800-869-1123 (toll-free in GA)

Hawaii

State Offices

Executive Director, Office of Consumer
Protection
Dept. of Commerce and Consumer Affairs
235 S. Beretania St., Rm. 801
PO Box 3767
Honolulu, HI 96813-3767
808-586-2636

Investigator, Office of Consumer
Protection
Dept. of Commerce and Consumer Affairs
75 Aupuni St.
Hilo, HI 96720
808-974-6230

Investigator, Office of Consumer Protection
Dept. of Commerce and Consumer Affairs
54 High St.
P.O. Box 1098
Wailuku, HI 96793
808-984-8244

Idaho

State Office

Deputy Attorney General
Office of the Attorney General
Consumer Protection Unit
650 W. State Street
Boise, ID 83720-0010
208-334-2424
800-432-3545 (toll-free in ID)

Illinois

State Offices

Attorney General
Governor's Office of Citizens Assistance
222 S. College
Springfield, IL 62706
217-782-0244
800-642-3112

Chief, Consumer Protection Division
Office of the Attorney General
100 W. Randolph St., 12th Fl.
Chicago, IL 60601
312-814-3000
TDD: 312-793-2852

Bureau Chief
Consumer Fraud Bureau
100 W. Randolph St., 13th Fl.
Chicago, IL 60601
312-814-3580
TDD: 312-814-3374
800-386-5438 (toll-free in IL)

Regional Offices

Assistant Attorney General
Carbondale Regional Office
Office of the Attorney General
1001 E. Main Professional Park East
Carbondale, IL 62901
618-457-3505
618-457-4421 (TDD)

Assistant Attorney General
Champaign Regional Office
34 E. Main St.
Champaign, IL 61820
217-333-7691 (voice/TDD)
800-243-0618 (toll-free)

Assistant Attorney General and Chief
Consumer Fraud Bureau
Office of the Attorney General
500 S. Second St.
Springfield, IL 62706
217-782-9020
800-252-8666 (toll-free in IL)
800-386-5438 (toll-free in Chicago)

County Offices

Supervisor, Consumer Fraud Division-303
Cook County Office of the State's Attorney
303 Daley Center
Chicago, IL 60602
312-345-2400

State's Attorney
Madison County Office of the State's Attorney
157 N. Main, Ste. 402
Edwardsville, IL 62025
618-692-6280

City Offices

Commissioner, Chicago Dept. of
   Consumer Services
121 N. LaSalle St., Rm. 808
Chicago, IL 60602
312-744-4006
312-744-9385 (TDD)

Administrator, Des Plaines Consumer
  Protection Commission
1420 Miner St.
Des Plaines, IL 60016
847-391-5378

Indiana

State Office

Chief Counsel and Director
Consumer Protection Division
Office of the Attorney General
Indiana Gov't Center S., 5th Fl.
402 W. Washington St.
Indianapolis, IN 46204
317-232-6330
800-382-5516 (toll-free in IN)

County Office

Marion County Prosecuting Attorney
560 City-County Building
200 E. Washington St.
Indianapolis, IN 46204-3363
317-327-5338

Iowa

State Office

Assistant Attorney General
Consumer Protection Division
Office of the Attorney General
1300 E. Walnut St., 2nd Fl.
Des Moines, IA 50319
515-281-5926

Kansas

State Office

Deputy Attorney General
Consumer Protection Division
Office of the Attorney General
301 W. 10th
Kansas Judicial Center

Topeka, KS 66612-1597
913-296-3751
800-432-2310 (toll-free in KS)

County Office

Head, Consumer Fraud Division
Johnson County District Attorney's Office
Johnson County Courthouse
PO Box 728
Olathe, KS 66051
913-764-8484, ext. 5287

City Office

City Attorney's Office
215 S.E. 7th St.
Topeka, KS 66603
913-368-3885

Kentucky

State Offices

Director, Consumer Protection Division
Office of the Attorney General
1024 Capital Center Dr.
PO Box 2000
Frankfort, KY 40601-2000
502-573-2200

Administrator, Consumer Protection Division
Office of the Attorney General
107 S. 4th St.
Louisville, KY 40202
502-595-3262

Louisiana

State Office

Chief, Consumer Protection Section
Office of the Attorney General
1 America Pl.
PO Box 94095
Baton Rouge, LA 70804-9095
504-342-9638

County Office

Chief, Consumer Protection Division
Jefferson Parish District Attorney's Office
5th Floor, Gretna Courthouse Annex
Gretna, LA 70053
504-364-3644

Maine

State Offices

Director, Office of Consumer Regulation
State House Station
Augusta, ME 04333-0035
207-624-8527
800-332-8529 (toll-free in ME)

Chief, Consumer and Antitrust Division
Office of the Attorney General
State House Station No. 6
Augusta, ME 04333
207-626-8849 (9 AM–1 PM)

Maryland

State Offices

Chief, Consumer Protection Division
Office of the Attorney General
200 St. Paul Pl.
Baltimore, MD 21202-2021
410-528-8662 (9 AM–3 PM)
410-576-6372 (TDD in Baltimore area)

Director, Licensing & Consumer Services
Motor Vehicle Administration
6601 Ritchie Hwy., N.E.
Glen Burnie, MD 21062
301-768-7535

Consumer Affairs Specialist
Eastern Shore Branch Office
Consumer Protection Division
Office of the Attorney General
201 Baptist St., Ste. 30

Salisbury, MD 21801-4976
410-543-6642

Director, Western Maryland Branch Office
Consumer Protection Division
Office of the Attorney General
138 E. Antietam St., Ste. 210
Hagerstown, MD 21740-5684
301-791-4780

County Offices

Administrator, Howard County Office of
    Consumer Affairs
6751 Columbia Gateway Dr.
Columbia, MD 21046
410-313-6420
410-313-6401 (TDD)

Acting Director, Montgomery County
    Office of Consumer Affairs
100 Maryland Ave., 3rd Fl.
Rockville, MD 20850
301-217-7373

Executive Director
Prince George's County Office of
    Business and Regulatory Affairs
County Administration Bldg., Ste. L15
Upper Marlboro, MD 20772
301-952-5323
301-925-5167 (TDD)

Massachusetts

State Offices

Chief, Consumer and Antitrust Division
Dept. of the Attorney General
1 Ashburton Place
Boston, MA 02108
617-727-2200
(information and referral to local
    consumer offices that work in
    conjunction with the Dept. of the
    Attorney General)

Secretary, Executive Office of Consumer
  Affairs and Business Regulation
One Ashburton Place, Rm. 1411
Boston, MA 02108
617-727-7780 (information and referral
  only)

Assistant Attorney, Western Massachusetts
  Consumer Protection Division
Dept. of the Attorney General
436 Dwight St.
Springfield, MA 01103
413-784-1240

County Offices

Case Coordinator
Consumer Fraud Prevention
North Western District Attorney's Office
238 Main St.
Greenfield, MA 01301
413-774-5102

Director, Consumer Fraud Prevention
Hampshire County District Attorney's
  Office
1 Court Square
Northhampton, MA 01060
413-586-9225

Director
Consumer Council of Worcester County
484 Main St., 2nd Floor
Worcester, MA 01608-1690
508-754-1176

City Offices

Commissioner, Mayor's Office of
  Consumer Affairs and Licensing
Boston City Hall, Rm. 817
Boston, MA 02201
617-635-4165

Director, Consumer Information Center
Springfield Action Commission
PO Box 1449 Main Office

Springfield, MA 01101
413-263-6513
(Hampton and Hampshire Counties)

Michigan

State Offices

Assistant in Charge
Consumer Protection Division
Office of the Attorney General
PO Box 30213
Lansing, MI 48909
517-373-1140

Director
Bureau of Automotive Regulation
Michigan Dept. of State
Lansing, MI 48918-1200
517-373-4777
800-292-4204 (toll-free in MI)

County Offices

Chief Investigator
Bay County Consumer Protection Unit
Bay County Building
Bay City, MI 48708-5994
517-895-4139

Director, Consumer Protection Dept.
Macomb County
Office of the Prosecuting Attorney
Macomb Court Building, 6th Fl.
Mt. Clemens, MI 48043
810-469-5350
810-466-8714 (TDD)

City Office

Director, City of Detroit
Dept. of Consumer Affairs
1600 Cadillac Tower
Detroit, MI 48226
313-224-3508

Minnesota

State Office

Director, Consumer Services Division
Office of the Attorney General
1400 NCL Tower, 445 Minnesota St.
St. Paul, MN 55101
612-296-3353

County Office

Citizen Protection Unit
Hennepin County Attorney's Office
C-2000 County Government Center
Minneapolis, MN 55487
612-348-4528

City Office

Director
Minneapolis Dept. of Licenses &
    Consumer Services
One C City Hall
Minneapolis, MN 55415
612-673-2080

Mississippi

State Offices

Special Assistant Attorney General
Director, Office of Consumer Protection
PO Box 22947
Jackson, MS 39225-2947
601-359-4231
800-281-4418 (toll-free in MS)

Director, Bureau of Regulatory Services
Dept. of Agriculture and Commerce
121 N. Jefferson St.
PO Box 1609
Jackson, MS 39201
601-354-7063

Missouri

State Office

Chief Counsel, Consumer Protection Division
Office of the Attorney General
PO Box 899
Jefferson City, MO 65102
573-751-3321
800-392-8222 (toll-free in MO)

Montana

State Office

Chief Legal Counsel, Consumer Affairs Unit
Dept. of Commerce
1424 Ninth Ave.
Box 200501
Helena, MT 59620-0501
406-444-4312

Nebraska

State Office

Assistant Attorney General
Consumer Protection Division
Dept. of Justice
2115 State Capitol
PO Box 98920
Lincoln, NE 68509
402-471-2682

Nevada

State Offices

Commissioner of Consumer Affairs
Dept. of Business and Industry
1850 E. Sahara, Ste. 101
Las Vegas, NV 89158
702-486-7355
800-326-5202 (toll-free in NV)
702-486-7901 (TDD)

Supervisory Compliance Investigator
Consumer Affairs Division
Dept. of Business and Industry
4600 Kietzke Lane, B-113
Reno, NV 89502
702-688-1800
800-326-5202 (toll-free in NV)
702-486-7901 (TDD)

New Hampshire

State Office

Chief, Consumer Protection and Antitrust
  Bureau
Office of the Attorney General
33 Capitol St.
Concord, NH 03301
603-271-3641

New Jersey

State Offices

Director, Division of Consumer Affairs
124 Halsey St.
PO Box 45027
Newark, NJ 07101
201-504-6534

Deputy Attorney General
New Jersey Division of Law
PO Box 45029
124 Halsey St., 5th Fl.
Newark, NJ 07101
201-648-7579

County Offices

Director, Atlantic County Consumer
  Affairs
1333 Atlantic Ave., 8th Fl.
Atlantic City, NJ 08401
609-345-6700

Director, Bergen County Division of
  Consumer Protection
21 Main St., Rm. 101-E
Hackensack, NJ 07601-7000
201-646-2650

Director, Burlington County Office of
  Consumer Affairs
49 Rancocas Rd.
Mount Holly, NJ 08060
609-265-5058

Director, Camden County Office of
  Consumer Protection/Weights and
  Measures
Jefferson House
Lakeland Road
Blackwood, NJ 08012
609-374-6161

Director, Cape May County Consumer
  Affairs
4 Moore Road
Cape May Court House, NJ 08210
609-463-6475

Director, Cumberland County Dept. of
  Consumer Affairs and Weights and
  Measures
788 E. Commerce St.
Bridgeton, NJ 08302
609-453-2203

Sr. Contact Person, Essex County
  Consumer Services
15 South Munn Ave., 2nd Fl.
E. Orange, NJ 07018
201-678-8071
201-678-8928

Director, Gloucester County Dept. of
  Consumer Protection/Weights &
  Measures
152 N. Broad. St.
Woodbury, NJ 08096
609-853-3349
609-853-3358
609-848-6616 (TDD)

Director, Hudson County Division of
   Consumer Affairs
595 Newark Ave.
Jersey City, NJ 07306
201-795-6295

Director, Hunterdon County Consumer
   Affairs
PO Box 283
Lebanon, NJ 08833
908-236-2249

Division Chief
Mercer County Consumer Affairs
640 S. Broad St., Rm. 229
PO Box 8068
Trenton, NJ 08650-0068
609-989-6671

Director, Middlesex County Consumer Affairs
10 Corporate Place South
Piscataway, NJ 08854
908-463-6000
908-463-6008

Director, Monmouth County Consumer
   Affairs
50 E. Main St.
PO Box 1255
Freehold, NJ 07728-1255
908-431-7900

Director, Ocean County Consumer Affairs
1027 Hooper Ave., Bldg. 2
Toms River, NJ 08754-2191
908-929-2105
908-506-5330

Director, Passaic County Consumer Affairs
401 Grand, Rm. 532
Paterson, NJ 07505
201-881-4547

Somerset County Consumer Affairs
County Administration Building
PO Box 3000
Somerville, NJ 08876-1262
908-231-7000, ext. 7400

Director, Union County Consumer Affairs
300 North Ave. East
PO Box 186
Westfield, NJ 07091
201-654-9840

City Offices

Director, Cinnaminson Consumer Affairs
Municipal Building
PO Box 2100
1621 Riverton Rd.
Cinnaminson, NJ 08077
609-829-6000

Director, Clark Consumer Affairs
430 Westfield Ave.
Clark, NJ 07066
908-388-3600

Director, Elizabeth Consumer Affairs
City Hall
50-60 W. Scott Plaza
Elizabeth, NJ 07201
908-820-4183

Director, Livingston Consumer Affairs
357 S. Livingston Ave.
Livingston, NJ 07039
201-535-7976

Director, Maywood Consumer Affairs
459 Maywood Ave.
Maywood, NJ 07607
201-845-2900
201-845-5749

Director, Middlesex Borough Consumer
   Affairs
1200 Mountain Ave.
Middlesex, NJ 08846
908-356-8090

Director, Mountainside Consumer Affairs
1455 Coles Ave.
Mountainside, NJ 07092
908-232-6600

Deputy Mayor, Director Consumer Affairs
Municipal Building
4233 Kennedy Blvd.
N. Bergen, NJ 07047
210-392-2157
201-330-7291
201-330-7292

Director, Nutley Consumer Affairs
Public Safety Building
228 Chestnut St.
Nutley, NJ 07110
201-284-4936

Investigator, Perth Amboy Consumer Affairs
City Hall
1 Olive St.
Perth Amboy, NJ 08861 ·
908-826-0290, ext. 72

Director, Plainfield Action Services
510 Watchtung Ave.
Plainfield, NJ 07060
908-753-3519

Director, Secaucus Dept. of Consumer
   Affairs
Municipal Government Center
Secaucus, NJ 07094
201-330-2019

Director, Union Township Consumer Affairs
Municipal Building
1976 Morris Ave.
Union, NJ 07083
908-688-6763

Director, Wayne Township Consumer
   Affairs
475 Valley Rd.
Wayne, NJ 07470
201-694-1800, ext. 3290

Director, Weehawken Consumer Affairs
400 Park Ave.
Weehawken, NJ 07087
201-319-6005

Woodbridge Consumer Affairs
Municipal Building
One Main Street
Woodbridge, NJ 07095
908-634-4500, ext. 6058

New Mexico

State Office

Consumer Protection Division
Office of the Attorney General
PO Drawer 1508
Santa Fe, NM 87504
505-827-6060
800-678-1508 (toll-free in NM)

New York

State Offices

Deputy Chief, Bureau of Consumer Fraud
   and Protection
Office of the Attorney General
State Capitol
Albany, NY 12224
518-474-5481
800-771-7755 (toll-free hotline)

Chairperson and Executive Director
New York State Consumer Protection
   Board
5 Empire State Plaza, Ste. 2101
Albany, NY 12223-1556
518-474-8583

Assistant Attorney General
Bureau of Consumer Fraud and Protection
Office of the Attorney General
120 Broadway
New York, NY 10271
212-416-8345
212-416-8940 (TDD)
800-771-7755 (toll-free)

Regional Offices

Assistant Attorney General in Charge
Central New York Regional Office
44 Hawley St., 17th Fl.
State Office Bldg.
Binghamton, NY 13901
607-721-8779

Assistant Attorney General in Charge
Buffalo Regional Office
Office of the Attorney General
65 Court St.
Buffalo, NY 14202
716-847-7184
800-771-7755 (toll-free)

Assistant Attorney General in Charge
Poughkeepsie Regional Office
Office of the Attorney General
235 Main St.
Poughkeepsie, NY 12601
914-485-3920
800-771-7755 (toll-free)

Assistant Attorney General in Charge
Rochester Regional Office
Office of the Attorney General
144 Exchange Blvd.
Rochester, NY 14614
716-546-7430
716-327-3249 (TDD)
800-771-7755 (toll-free)

Assistant Attorney General in Charge
Suffolk Regional Office
Office of the Attorney General
300 Motor Pkwy.
Hauppauge, NY 11788
516-231-2400

Assistant Attorney General in Charge
Syracuse Regional Office
Office of the Attorney General
615 Erie Blvd. West, Ste. 102
Syracuse, NY 13204-2465
315-448-4848
800-771-7755

Assistant Attorney General in Charge
Utica Regional Office
Office of the Attorney General
207 Genesee St.
Utica, NY 13501
315-793-2225
315-793-2228
800-771-7755 (toll-free)

County Offices

Director, Dutchess County Dept. of
    Consumer Affairs
38-A Dutchess Turnpike
Poughkeepsie, NY 12603
914-486-2947

Assistant District Attorney
Consumer Fraud Bureau
Erie County District Attorney's Office
25 Delaware Ave.
Buffalo, NY 14202
716-858-2424

Commissioner, Nassau County Office of
    Consumer Affairs
160 Old Country Rd.
Mineola, NY 11501
516-571-2600

Executive Director
New Justice Conflict Resolution Services
    Inc.
1153 W. Fayette St., Ste. 301
Syracuse, NY 13204
315-471-4676

District Attorney, Orange County District
    Attorney's Office
255 Main St.
County Gov't Center
Goshen, NY 10924
914-294-5471

Commissioner
Rockland County Office of Consumer
    Protection

County Office Building
18 New Hempstead Rd.
New City, NY 10956
914-638-5280

Director, Steuben County Dept. of Weights,
Measures and Consumer Affairs
3 E. Pulteney Square
Bath, NY 14810
607-776-9631
607-776-9631, ext. 2406 (voice/TDD)

Commissioner, Suffolk County
Executive's Office of Consumer Affairs
N. County Complex, Bldg. 340
Veterans Memorial Highway
Hauppauge, NY 11788
516-853-4600

Director, Ulster County Consumer Fraud
Bureau
PO Box 1800
Kingston, NY 12402
914-339-5680

Chief, Frauds Bureau
Westchester County
District Attorney's Office
111 Grove St.
White Plains, NY 10601
914-285-3414

Deputy Director, Westchester County
Dept. of Consumer Protection
112 E. Post Rd., 4th Fl.
White Plains, NY 10601
914-285-3155

City Offices

Citizen Advocate, Office of Citizen
Services
Babylon Town Hall
200 E. Sunrise Highway
281 Phelps Lane
Lindenhurst, NY 11757
516-957-7474

Town of Colonie Consumer Protection
Memorial Town Hall
Newtonville, NY 12128
518-783-2790

Commissioner, Mt. Vernon Office of
Consumer Protection
City Hall
Mt. Vernon, NY 10550
914-665-2433

Commissioner, New York City Dept. of
Consumer Affairs
42 Broadway
New York, NY 10004
212-487-4401
212-487-4465 (TDD)

Director, Queens Neighborhood Office
New York City Dept. of Consumer Affairs
120-55 Queens Blvd., Rm. 301A
Kew Gardens, NY 11424
718-261-2990

Schenectady Bureau of Consumer Protection
City Hall, Rm. 204
Jay St.
Schenectady, NY 12305
518-382-5061

Director, Yonkers Office of Consumer
Protection, Weights and Measures
201 Palisade Ave.
Yonkers, NY 10703
914-377-6807

North Carolina

State Office

Special Deputy Attorney General
Consumer Protection Section
Office of the Attorney General
Raney Building
PO Box 629
Raleigh, NC 27602
919-733-7741

North Dakota

State Offices

Office of the Attorney General
600 E. Blvd. Ave.
Bismarck, ND 58505
701-224-2210
800-472-2600 (toll-free in ND)

Director, Consumer Fraud Section
Office of the Attorney General
600 E. Blvd. Ave.
Bismarck, ND 58505
701-224-3404
800-472-2600 (toll-free in ND)

County Office

Executive Director
Community Action Agency
1013 N. 5th St.
Grand Forks, ND 58201
701-746-5431

Ohio

State Offices

Consumer Frauds and Crimes Section
Office of the Attorney General
30 E. Broad. St.
State Office Tower, 25th Fl.
Columbus, OH 43266-0410
614-466-4986 (complaints)
614-466-1393 (TDD)
800-282-0515 (toll-free in OH)

Office of Consumers' Counsel
77 S. High St., 15th Fl.
Columbus, OH 43266-0550
614-466-9605 (voice/TDD)
800-282-9448 (toll-free in OH)

County Offices

Director, Corrupt Activities Protection Unit
Franklin County Office of Prosecuting
    Attorney
369 S. High St.
Columbus, OH 43215
614-462-3555

Assistant Prosecuting Attorney
Montgomery County Fraud and Economic
    Crimes Division
301 W. 3rd St.
Dayton Montgomery County Courts
    Building
Dayton, OH 45402
513-225-4747

Prosecuting Attorney
Portage County Office of the Prosecuting
    Attorney
466 S. Chestnut St.
Ravenna, OH 44266-3000
216-296-4593

Prosecuting Attorney
Summit County Office of the Prosecuting
    Attorney
53 University Ave.
Akron, OH 44308-1680
330-643-2800

City Offices

Department of Neighborhood Services
Division of Human Services
City Hall, Rm. 126
801 Plum St.
Cincinnati, OH 45202
513-352-3971

Director, Youngstown Office of Consumer
    Affairs and Weights and Measures
26 S. Phelps St.
City Hall
Youngstown, OH 44503-1318
216-742-8884

Oklahoma

State Offices

Assistant Attorney General
Office of the Attorney General
4545 Lincoln Blvd., Ste. 260
Oklahoma City, OK 73105
405-521-4274
405-521-2029 (consumer hotline)

Administrator, Dept. of Consumer Credit
4545 Lincoln Blvd., Ste. 104
Oklahoma City, OK 73105-3408
405-521-3653

Oregon

State Office

Attorney in Charge
Financial Fraud Section
Dept. of Justice
1162 Court St. N.E.
Salem, OR 97310
503-378-4732

Pennsylvania

State Offices

Director, Bureau of Consumer Protection
Office of the Attorney General
Strawberry Square, 14th Fl.
Harrisburg, PA 17120
717-787-9707
800-441-2555 (toll-free in PA)

Consumer Advocate
Office of Consumer Advocate–Utilities
Office of the Attorney General
1425 Strawberry Square
Harrisburg, PA 17120
717-783-5048 (utilities only)

Deputy Attorney General
Bureau of Consumer Protection
Office of the Attorney General
1251 S. Cedar Crest Blvd., Ste. 309
Allentown, PA 18103
215-821-6690

Director, Bureau of Consumer Services
Pennsylvania Public Utility Commission
PO Box 3265
203 N. Office Building
Harrisburg, PA 17105-3265
717-787-1740
800-782-1110 (toll-free in PA)

Deputy Attorney General
Bureau of Consumer Protection
Office of the Attorney General
919 State St., Rm. 203
Erie, PA 16501
814-871-4371

Sr. Deputy Attorney General
Bureau of Consumer Protection
Office of the Attorney General
171 Lovell Ave., Ste. 202
Ebensburg, PA 15931
814-949-7900
800-4412555 (toll-free in PA)

Deputy Attorney General
Bureau of Consumer Protection
Office of the Attorney General
21 S. 12th St., 2nd Fl.
Philadelphia, PA 19107
215-560-2414
800-441-2555 (toll-free in PA)

Deputy Attorney General
Bureau of Consumer Protection
Office of the Attorney General
Manor Complex, 6th Fl.
564 Forbes Ave.
Pittsburgh, PA 15219
412-565-5394
800-441-2555 (toll-free in PA)

Deputy Attorney General
Bureau of Consumer Protection
Office of the Attorney General
214 Samters Bldg.
101 Penn Ave.
Scranton, PA 18503-2025
717-963-4913

Regional Office
Office of the Attorney General
Bureau of Consumer Protection
132 Kline Village
Harrisburg, PA 17104
717-787-7109

County Offices

Director, Beaver County Alliance for
    Consumer Protection
699 Fifth St.
Beaver, PA 15009-1997
412-728-7267

Director/Chief Sealer, Bucks County
    Consumer Protection, Weights and
    Measures
50 N. Main
Doylestown, PA 18901
215-348-7442

Director, Chester County Bureau of
    Consumer Protection, Weights and
    Measures
Government Services Center, Ste. 390
601 Westtown Rd.
West Chester, PA 19382-4547
610-344-6150
800-692-1100 (toll-free in PA)

Consumer Mediator, Cumberland County
    Consumer Affairs
One Courthouse Square
Carlisle, PA 17013-3330
717-240-6180

Director, Delaware County Office of
    Consumer Affairs, Weights and
    Measures
Government Center Building
Second and Olive Sts.
Media, PA 19063
610-891-4865

Director, Montgomery County Consumer
    Affairs Dept.
County Courthouse
Norristown, PA 19404
610-278-3565

City Office

Chief, Economic Crime Unit
Philadelphia District Attorney's Office
1421 Arch St.
Philadelphia, PA 19102
215-686-8750

Puerto Rico

Secretary, Dept. of Consumer Affairs
    (DACO)
Minillas Station, PO Box 41059
Santurce, PR 00940-1059
787-721-0940
787-726-6570

Secretary, Dept. of Justice
PO Box 192
San Juan, PR 00902
787-721-2900

Rhode Island

State Offices

President, Consumer Credit Counseling
    Service
535 Centerville Rd., Ste. 103
Warwick, RI 02886
401-732-1800
800-781-2227 (toll-free in RI)

Director, Consumer Protection Division
Dept. of the Attorney General
72 Pine St.
Providence, RI 02903
401-274-4400
401-453-0410 (TDD)
800-852-7776 (toll-free in RI)

South Carolina

State Offices

Sr. Assistant Attorney General
Consumer Fraud and Antitrust Section
Office of the Attorney General
PO Box 11549
Columbia, SC 29211
803-734-3970

Administrator, Consumer Advocate
Dept. of Consumer Affairs
PO Box 5757
Columbia, SC 29250-5757
803-734-9452
803-734-9455 (TDD)
800-922-1594 (toll-free in SC)

State Ombudsman
Office of Executive Policy and Program
1205 Pendleton St., Rm. 308
Columbia, SC 29201
803-734-0457
803-734-1147 (TDD)

South Dakota

State Office

Assistant Attorney General
Division of Consumer Affairs
Office of the Attorney General
500 E. Capitol
State Capitol Building
Pierre, SD 57501-5070
605-773-4400

Tennessee

State Offices

Deputy Attorney General
Antitrust and Consumer Protection
   Division
Office of the Attorney General
450 James Robertson Pkwy.
Nashville, TN 37243-0485
615-741-2672

Director, Division of Consumer Affairs
Dept. of Commerce and Insurance
500 James Robertson Pkwy., 5th Fl.
Nashville, TN 37243-0600
615-741-4737
800-342-8385 (toll-free in TN)
800-422-CLUB (toll-free health club
   hotline in TN)

Texas

State Offices

Assistant Attorney General and Chief,
   Consumer Protection Division
Office of the Attorney General
Supreme Court Building
PO Box 12548
Austin, TX 78711
512-463-2070

Assistant Attorney General
Consumer Protection Division
Office of the Attorney General
714 Jackson St., Ste. 700
Dallas, TX 75202-4506
214-742-8944

Assistant Attorney General
Consumer Protection Division
Office of the Attorney General
6090 Surety Dr., Rm. 260
El Paso, TX 79905
915-772-9476

Assistant Attorney General
Consumer Protection Division
Office of the Attorney General
1019 Congress St., Ste. 1550
Houston, TX 77002-1702
713-223-5886

Assistant Attorney General
Consumer Protection Division
Office of the Attorney General
1208 14th St., Ste. 900
Lubbock, TX 79401-3997
806-747-5238

Assistant Attorney General
Consumer Protection Division
Office of the Attorney General
3600 N. 23rd St., Ste. 305
McAllen, TX 78501-1685
512-682-4547

Assistant Attorney General
Consumer Protection Division
Office of the Attorney General
115 E. Travis St., Ste. 925
San Antonio, TX 78205-1607
512-225-4191

Office of Consumer Protection
State Board of Insurance
816 Congress Ave., Ste. 1400
Austin, TX 78701-2430
512-322-4143

County Office

Assistant District Attorney and Chief of
   Dallas County District Attorney's
   Office
Specialized Crime Division
133 N. Industrial Blvd., LB 19
Dallas, TX 75207-4313
214-653-3820

Assistant District Attorney and Chief
   Harris County Consumer Fraud
   Division
Office of the District Attorney
201 Fannin, Ste. 200
Houston, TX 77002-1901
713-221-5836

City Office

Director, Dallas Consumer Protection
   Division
Health and Human Services Dept.
320 E. Jefferson Blvd., Ste. 312
Dallas, TX 75203
214-948-4400

Utah

State Offices

Director, Division of Consumer Protection
Dept. of Commerce
160 E. 3rd S.
PO Box 45802
Salt Lake City, UT 84145-0802
801-530-6601

Assistant Attorney General for Consumer
   Affairs
Office of the Attorney General
115 State Capitol
Salt Lake City, UT 84114
801-538-1331

Vermont

State Offices

Assistant Attorney General and Chief,
   Public Protection Division
Office of the Attorney General
109 State St.
Montpelier, VT 05609-1001
802-828-3171

Supervisor, Consumer Assurance Section
Dept. of Agriculture, Food and Market
120 State St.
Montpelier, VT 05620-2901
802-828-2436

Virgin Islands

Commissioner, Dept. of Licensing and
    Consumer Affairs
Consumer Affairs
Property and Procurement Building
Subbase #1, Rm. 205
St. Thomas, VI 00802
809-774-3130

Virginia

State Offices

Chief, Antitrust and Consumer Litigation
    Section
Office of the Attorney General
Supreme Court Building
101 N. Eighth St.
Richmond, VA 23219
804-786-2116
800-451-1525 (toll-free in VA)

Director, Division of Consumer Affairs
Dept. of Agriculture and Consumer
    Services
Rm. 101, Washington Building
1100 Bank St.
PO Box 1163
Richmond, VA 23219
804-786-2042

Investigator, Northern Virginia Branch
Office of Consumer Affairs
Dept. of Agriculture and Consumer
    Services
100 N. Washington St., Ste. 412
Falls Church, VA 22046
703-532-1613

County Offices

Section Chief, Office of Citizen and
    Consumer Affairs
#1 Court House Plaza, Ste. 314
2100 Clarendon Blvd.
Arlington, VA 22201
703-358-3260

Director, Fairfax County Dept. of
    Consumer Affairs
3959 Pender Dr., Ste. 200
Fairfax, VA 22030-6093
703-246-5949
703-591-3260 (TDD)

Administrator, Prince William County
    Office of Consumer Affairs
4370 Ridgewood Center Dr.
Prince William, VA 22192-9201
703-792-7370

City Offices

Director, Alexandria Office of Citizens'
    Assistance
City Hall
PO Box 178
Alexandria, VA 22313
703-838-4350
703-838-5056 (TDD)

Coordinator, Division of Consumer Affairs
City Hall
Norfolk, VA 23501
804-441-2821
804-441-2000 (TDD)

Assistant to the City Manager
Roanoke Consumer Protection Division
364 Municipal Building
215 Church Ave., S.W.
Roanoke, VA 24011
703-981-2583

Director, Consumer Affairs Division
Office of the Commonwealth's Attorney
3500 Virginia Beach Blvd., Ste. 304
Virginia Beach, VA 23452
804-431-4610

Washington

State Offices

Investigator, Consumer and Business Fair
   Practices Division
Office of the Attorney General
111 Olympia Ave., N.E.
Olympia, WA 98501
206-753-6210

Director of Consumer Services
Consumer and Business Fair Practices
   Division
Office of the Attorney General
900 Fourth Ave., Ste. 2000
Seattle, WA 98164
206-464-6431
800-551-4636 (toll-free in WA)

Chief, Consumer and Business Fair
   Practices Division
Office of the Attorney General
W. 1116 Riverside Ave.
Spokane, WA 99201
509-456-3123

Contact Person, Consumer and Business
   Fair Practices Division
Office of the Attorney General
1019 Pacific Ave., 3rd Fl.
Tacoma, WA 98402-4411
206-593-2904

City Offices

Director, Dept. of Weights and Measures
3200 Cedar St.
Everett, WA 98201
206-259-8810

Chief Deputy Prosecuting Attorney
Fraud Division
1002 Bank of California
900 4th Ave.
Seattle, WA 98164
206-296-9010

Director, Seattle Dept. of Licenses and
   Consumer Affairs
102 Municipal Building
600 4th Ave.
Seattle, WA 98104-1893
206-684-8484

West Virginia

State Offices

Director, Consumer Protection Division
Office of the Attorney General
812 Quarrier St., 6th Fl.
Charleston, WV 25301
304-348-8986
800-368-8808 (toll-free in WV)

Director, Division of Weights and
   Measures
Dept. of Labor
1800 Washington St., East
Building #3, Rm. 319
Charleston, WV 25305
304-348-7890

City Office

Director, Dept. of Consumer Protection
PO Box 2749
Charleston, WV 25330
304-348-8172

Wisconsin

State Offices

Administrator, Division of Trade and
    Consumer Protection
Dept. of Agriculture, Trade and Consumer
    Protection
801 W. Badger Rd.
PO Box 8911
Madison, WI 53708
608-266-9836
800-422-7128 (toll-free in WI)

Regional Supervisor, Division of Trade
    and Consumer Protection
Dept. of Agriculture, Trade and Consumer
    Protection
927 Loring St.
Altoona, WI 54720
715-839-3848
800-422-7218 (toll-free in WI)

Regional Supervisor, Division of Trade
    and Consumer Protection
Dept. of Agriculture, Trade and Consumer
    Protection
200 N. Jefferson St., Ste. 146A
Green Bay, WI 54301
414-448-5111
800-422-7128 (toll-free in WI)

Regional Supervisor, Consumer Protection
    Regional Office
Dept. of Agriculture, Trade and Consumer
    Protection
3333 N. Mayfair Rd., Ste. 114
Milwaukee, WI 53222-3288
414-257-8956

Assistant Attorney General
Office of Consumer Protection and Citizen
    Advocacy
Dept. of Justice
PO Box 7856
Madison, WI 53707-7856
608-266-1852
800-362-8189 (toll-free)

Assistant Attorney General
Office of Consumer Protection
Dept. of Justice
Milwaukee State Office Building
819 N. 6th St., Rm. 520
Milwaukee, WI 53203-1678
414-227-4948
800-362-8189 (toll-free)

County Offices

District Attorney
Marathon County District Attorney's
    Office
Marathon County Courthouse
Wausau, WI 54401
715-847-5555

Assistant District Attorney
Milwaukee County District Attorney's
    Office
Consumer Fraud Unit
821 W. State St., Rm. 412
Milwaukee, WI 53233-1485
414-278-4792

Consumer Fraud Investigator
Racine County Sheriff's Dept.
717 Wisconsin Ave.
Racine, WI 53403
414-636-3125

Wyoming

State Office

Assistant Attorney General
Office of the Attorney General
123 State Capitol Building
Cheyenne, WY 82002
307-777-7874

Information in this section was taken from
the Consumers' Resource Handbook, 1992
edition, U.S. Office of Consumer Affairs.

GLOSSARY

annual percentage rate (APR) The percentage rate, reported as a yearly rate.

applicant Any person who requests credit from a creditor.

asset Property that can be used to repay a debt such as cash, real estate, or personal property.

balance The amount owed on an account.

bankruptcy The act of having your estate administered under the bankruptcy laws for the benefit of the creditors.

better business bureau A company that tracks the activity of businesses and reports to the public on request if there have been any complaints.

charge card An instrument used to buy goods and services from the issuing merchant on credit; payment usually is due in 30 days.

collateral Property that is offered to secure a loan or credit; it becomes subject to seizure in the case of default.

cosigner Another individual who signs for a loan and assumes equal liability for the debt.

credit The promise to pay in the future in order to buy or borrow in the present; a sum of money due a person or business.

credit card An instrument that may be used repeatedly to borrow money or purchase goods and services on credit.

credit contract A written agreement between the creditor and debtor that enforces the terms of the contract.

credit history A record of how a person has repaid debts.

credit rating   An evaluation by a creditor or credit reporting agency to reflect a debtor's credit history based on payment pattern.

credit reporting agency   A company that keeps credit records on individuals.

creditor   An individual or business who makes credit available by lending money or selling goods and services for credit.

default   The failure to meet a financial obligation.

deferred payment   A debt that can be paid at a later time.

deficiency   The difference between the amount you owe a creditor who has foreclosed on your house or repossessed an item of personal property—such as a car, and the amount of money the sale of the property brings in. This deficiency amount is owed to the creditor by the original debtor.

exempt   An account that can be released from obligation to pay in a bankruptcy.

finance charge   The dollar amount paid to get credit.

foreclosure   The right of a creditor, such as a mortgage lender that has a lien on your property, to force a sale of your property if you have stopped making payments to recover what is owed.

gross income   Your wages before taxes and expenses are taken out.

installment contract   A written agreement to pay for goods or service purchases. It sets forth the terms, such as the payments of principal and interest, and dates of payments.

joint account   An account that two or more people can use with all assuming the liability to repay the debt.

judgment   A judgment is the decision issued by a court at the end of a lawsuit. When there is a judgment against you, the court will indicate the total amount due the plaintiff (the one who sued you).

late payment   A payment made after the due date.

lien   The legal right to hold property or to have it sold or applied for the payment of a claim owed to a creditor. A lien is usually placed on real estate.

liquidate   To convert an asset to cash.

net income   The amount of money left from your paycheck after taxes and expenses are paid.

refinance   To pay old debts with a new loan.

reinstate a contract   If you fall behind in making your payments, and the property or item is foreclosed or repossessed, you have a period of time to get the property or item back. The property or item would then be restored to you after all the back payments and fees were brought current.

repossession   When a creditor reclaims or takes back property from a debtor who does not fulfill the terms of his/her contract.

retail credit   Credit offered to customers by merchants for the purpose of allowing them to buy now and pay later.

secured credit card   A credit card you can obtain by opening up a savings account with a bank offering this program. The bank will issue a major credit card and secure it with your deposit.

secured debt   A secured debt is a specific item used as collateral to guarantee payment. If the payments cease, the creditor is entitled to the item designated as collateral.

security agreement   A security agreement is the contract you sign when you get a secured loan. The agreement indicates what property or collateral can be seized should you default.

service charge   A fee charged for a particular service, often in addition to the interest charge.

unsecured debt   A debt which has no collateral linked to the debt; i.e., there is no specific item which is guaranteed. If the debt is not paid, the creditor must sue you to try and collect.

INDEX

ABOUT THE AUTHOR

Deborah McNaughton is the founder of Professional Credit Counselors. She is a nationally known credit expert who has been interviewed on hundreds of radio and television talk shows. McNaughton's business offers assistance in credit consulting, mortgages, real estate purchases, automobile purchases, and financial planning. She is the author of several books on credit including *The Insiders Guide to Managing Your Credit, Everything You Need to Know about Credit, Fix Your Credit, Have a Good Report* (which she coauthored with John Avanzini), and *The Credit Repair System,* a business opportunity manual that has helped hundreds of credit counseling businesses throughout the United States get started. McNaughton conducts credit and financial strategies seminars nationally and offers a distributor program for her seminars. In 1990, McNaughton founded Inner-Strength International, introducing her motivational workshop and manual "Yes You Can" to help individuals discover their full potential in life by focusing on finances, hope, and encouragement.

To receive more information about McNaughton's seminars, products, and services, write:

Deborah McNaughton
1100 Irvine Boulevard #541
Tustin, CA 92780
or call:
714-541-2637